WINDOW
ON AMERICA

BY EDWARD STREETER

Published on the occasion of the

175th Anniversary of

THE BANK OF NEW YORK

48 Wall Street, New York, N. Y.

Contents

	PAGE
FOREWORD	5

Chapter I (1783-1800)

THE FOUNDATIONS ARE LAID   9

Chapter II (1800-1851)

THE NATION BUILDERS   32

Chapter III (1851-1865)

THE GREAT EXPERIMENT ENDANGERED   55

Chapter IV (1865-1914)

THE EMERGENCE OF MODERN AMERICA   67

Chapter V (1914-1950)

CHANGING AMERICA   96

Chapter VI (1950-1959)

THRESHOLD OF A NEW WORLD   119

Foreword

The Bank of New York was organized March 15, 1784, only 110 days after the last boat-load of British troops had pulled away from the docks of Manhattan. It was present at the birth of a nation and has seen that nation emerge as a world power in the short space of 175 years.

The very speed with which the young Republic grew assured it of a turbulent history. The Bank of New York, during the course of its business life, has lived through six major panics, ten economic depressions, and has seen the country shaken by seven wars. In spite of these recurrent crises, however, the Bank has paid dividends each year throughout the period, largely because, in spite of the speculative temptations offered by a mushrooming economy, it has never deviated from the sound fiscal policies laid down by its founders.

When the Bank started, the new Republic was surrounded by a hostile world—one which was beginning to look acquisitively at the great, unexplored territory west of the Appalachians. Those early days seem so remote in this mechanized age as to lack reality and yet the intervening years could be spanned quite easily by three lives. It is the *change* that has taken place, rather than the time elapsed, which makes the gap appear so great.

Constant change has been the keynote of the American story from the outset. It was an atmosphere which called for maximum adaptability on the part of its bankers and its business men. The Revolution caused the people of the United States to break with the traditions of the old world. After 1783 they faced west for the first time rather than east and, when they found themselves confronted with problems to which past experience gave no answer, they learned to improvise.

The history of the Bank is inextricably woven into the broader history of the nation. It first opened its doors for business in a town of less than 22,000 inhabitants. It lived anxiously through the early days of the Republic, when no one could be certain that this bold experiment in democracy would survive. It watched the nation-builders pushing ceaselessly westward across the plains and over the gale-swept passes of the Rockies. It endured the agonies of civil war. And during the last half of the nineteenth century it witnessed the emergence of modern America, the growth of its corporations and the development of its technical knowledge.

Today its main office stands only a few blocks from its first home, but the provincial town in which it started has grown into a vast metropolis and the rural seaboard nation of 1784 has stretched across a continent and become the leader of the free world.

∘◯∘

On this, the 175th anniversary of its founding, The Bank of New York wishes to acknowledge its indebtedness to the City which gave it being and to the Nation in whose development it has been privileged to play a part.

WALTON HOUSE

CHAPTER I

The Foundations Are Laid
1783-1800

Shortly after one o'clock on the afternoon of November 25, 1783, Major General Henry Knox, Washington's youthful Chief of Artillery, led a detachment of troops down lower Broadway and took over Fort George, just south of Bowling Green, from a tight-lipped British officer.

It was a simple ceremony, quickly performed. The officer barked a command and the red-coated, white-gaitered soldiers drawn up before the entrance to the Fort marched off in the direction of Whitehall Slip where the last of England's army of occupation was being transferred in longboats to the waiting transports.

General Knox hurried back to report to Washington who was stationed with his staff about a half mile north of present City Hall. New York Harbor was a forest of masts and yardarms. The waters of the Upper Bay were swarming with small craft, either assisting in the embarkation or out to watch the evacuation of a hostile army. A few lumbering transports had already weighed anchor and their square sails were silhouetted against the afternoon sun as they moved slowly oceanward through the Narrows.

The American Revolution was over.

In spite of the fact that not a shot had been fired within its boundaries, seven years of occupation had left New York a devastated city.

Fire had broken out at the lower end of the island less than a week after the British troops moved in. Whipped by a near gale, it had destroyed the area west of Broad Street as far north as Beaver Street. At that point a shift in the wind had turned it westward to the Hudson. Destroying Trinity Church on its way, it had swept up the river until stopped by the grounds of King's College (present Columbia), then located just above Park Place.

During the war years there had been little incentive to rebuild the burned-over district which was still a no man's-land of broken masonry and blackened chimneys. In the areas spared by the fire, public buildings and churches had been used as military offices, prisons, hospitals, warehouses and even riding halls, until they were so battered that little of value remained except the outside walls.

The houses of the patriots who had fled from the city to escape the British had been stripped of everything usable. Streets had been allowed to fall into such disrepair that many were almost impassable. Trees had been cut and fences broken up for firewood and pre-Revolutionary gardens had reverted to jungles of weeds. The City's trade had been all but destroyed. Its treasury was empty. Only a courageous imagination could have visualized it as a world center in less than ten decades.

New York City had no monopoly on difficulties, however. From Maine to Georgia the new-born nation was faced with problems, external and internal, which might have been overwhelming had communications not been so bad that their magnitude and complexity were neither fully revealed nor appreciated.

The population of the United States at the end of the Revolution was approximately three and a quarter million — a figure comparable to that of the present boroughs of Manhattan and the Bronx combined. It was split into three areas so conditioned by climate, occupation and social background that they had few characteristics in common and even less common understanding.

Its frontiers lay in the spruce forests of southern Maine, along the mountains of New Hampshire and Vermont, among the stump-dotted clearings of the Mohawk Valley and the blue ridges of the Appalachians and through the pine forests of Georgia.

These were the front lines of American civilization. Beyond them lay the wilderness, unknown, untouched, its boundaries undefined.

o◯o

It was in this setting that The Bank of New York was born on March 15, 1784.

Considering the city's financial condition and the economic chaos that confronted the nation, the wonder is that such a major undertaking as the establishment of a bank could have been achieved so quickly. It was precisely because conditions *were* so chaotic, however, that banking facilities had become essential to the revival of the city's business life.

At the end of the Revolution hard money was understandably scarce. This situation was aggravated by the collapse of the bills of credit issued by the Continental Congress and the individual states during the war, which resulted in making specie the only acceptable legal tender. In order to transact business the immediate and pressing problem of the Government and the merchants was either to increase the supply of hard money or to devise some other medium of exchange.

Young Alexander Hamilton had been urging the creation of a "national" bank for a number of years. He had discussed the subject with Robert Morris of Philadelphia, who had also been thinking along similar lines, with the result that in December, 1781, the Bank of North America opened its offices in Philadelphia.

In spite of violent opposition the new venture was an immediate success. It was only natural, therefore, that as soon as the evacuation of the British was completed, steps should have been taken to establish a similar institution in New York.

At the outset there was basic disagreement as to the kind of bank that would best serve current needs. One faction, consisting mostly of landowners, wanted a "land bank," the capital of which would consist largely of real estate mortgages. Another group, with which Hamilton was associated, wanted a "money bank" whose capital would be entirely in specie.

Each faction tried to obtain an exclusive charter and each blocked the other. In the end, The Bank of New York was organized with a capital of $500,000 payable in gold or silver. Failing to obtain a charter it operated until 1791 under a constitution drawn up by Hamilton.

The new bank opened its offices on June 9, 1784, in the Walton House at 67 St. George's Square, also known as 156 Queen (present Pearl) Street. General Alexander McDougall, former naval officer, major general in Washington's Army, state senator and president of the New York State Society of the Cincinnati, became its first president and William Seton, a merchant, its cashier.

The Board of Directors was made up of well-to-do business men of the City; merchants such as Nicholas Low, who was also one of the largest owners of real estate both in the City and throughout the State; importers and shippers like Comfort Sands, who had made a fortune in the West Indian trade before he was thirty; business men like Robert Bowne whose firm, Bowne & Company, still operates under that name and whose family homestead, Bowne House, built in 1661, still stands in Flushing as a museum; manufacturers like Isaac Roosevelt, ancestor of Franklin D., who operated a sugar refinery across the street from the Bank.

It was Hamilton, however, who was most active in the organization of the Bank and in guiding it through its early stages. Brilliant, self-confident, industrious and blessed with seemingly inexhaustible energy, he left a lasting imprint on The Bank of New York as he did on almost everything that he touched.

He had long been a student of economics and was one

of the few men of the post-Revolutionary era who had a thorough grasp of banking principles. Professor W. G. Sumner in his *History of Banking* wrote of Hamilton's contribution, "The charter of The Bank of New York, which came from his hand, became the model on which numberless charters were afterwards constructed and . . . we must attribute to his opinions on banking a predominant influence in forming the banking institutions of this country."

o◯o

The adverse business conditions which existed when the Bank was founded, continued during the first few years of its life. The disruptions caused by seven years of war, the lack of specie and a stabilized currency, coupled with the handicap imposed by an almost powerless central government, made this inevitable.

At the beginning of 1788, interest on the internal and external debt of the nation exceeded national revenues. The currency was a hodgepodge of foreign coins, many of them clipped. The country was flooded with state and national paper money depreciating at different rates of speed. Small wonder the merchants did not know where to turn, or that Washington, with his flair for understatement, wrote to James Warren, "The wheels of government are clogged."

It is difficult for anyone accustomed to modern New York's overwhelming bigness to visualize the city in which The Bank of New York was founded. By present-day standards it scarcely deserved the name of city, its extreme northerly limits being less than a mile and half from present Battery Park.

In the better sections the houses were of red brick—two, or at most three stories in height. A few of the old Dutch houses still remained, the step-gabled ends of their sloping roofs facing the street. The principal streets were cobbled and must have been excessively noisy for there are frequent references in the newspapers of the day to their being closed with chains during church services and, in the neighborhood of City Hall, when Congress was in session.

A few of the old homes at the foot of Broadway had survived the fire and were still in use, but New York's fashionable residential district had already begun its northward march and at the end of the Revolution it was centered at the western end of Wall Street where Alexander Hamilton's house stood on the approximate site of the present New York Stock Exchange Building.

Present William Street was then the shopping center on which most of the dry-goods stores were located. General business was concentrated on Queen (present Pearl) and Water Streets. Here were the offices and business establishments of many of the men who were then or later associated with the Bank.

North of St. Paul's Chapel, Broadway became a dirt road which dwindled to a wagon track and eventually lost itself in a sheep pasture. The Chapel itself looked out across what was then known as "The Fields," an unkempt and dusty triangle at the north end of which, near the present site of City Hall, stood the Bridewell, which was the criminal prison, the Almshouse and the Debtors' Prison. From their barred windows the inmates were cheered by a view of the stocks, the whipping post and the gallows, the last being in frequent use in days when the death penalty was attached to such crimes as forgery, counterfeiting, rape, robbery, arson and "malicious maiming."

It was a city of contrasts where the mansions of the wealthy rubbed elbows with the shops of the tradesmen; where costly imported silks flounced unheeding over unswept and muddy street crossings and where the cult of gracious living was practised in the midst of sanitary conditions which would be considered unbearable by the most easygoing modern standards.

The water supply was insufficient and bad. There were wells and pumps in the middle of most of the streets, but the water which came from them was only fit for washing and was restricted even for that purpose by the labor of transporting it from the pumps to the houses. Drinking water was brought from sources north of the city in what were known as "tea-water carts," from which it was sold to householders by the gallon.

In spite of these handicaps the social life of the City was both gay and sophisticated. This was partly due to the fact that it was a federal and state capital until 1790 and 1796, respectively and also because post-Revolutionary New York was essentially a maritime city which gave it a world outlook that was reflected in the lavishness of its merchants' hospitality.

Philadelphia and Boston may have been more cultured,

but New York had an aggressiveness, an alertness and a drive which even then foretold the shape of things to come.

oⵔo

The affairs of men seldom remain static. Slowly, almost imperceptibly at first, the United States began to gain momentum. Up and down the coast from Boston to Savannah things were happening — some important, some trivial — the sum total of which accelerated the pace of recovery and influenced the direction that history was to take.

In New York, General Washington said goodby to his officers in Fraunces Tavern, thereby causing a sigh of relief from those who feared the influence of the military in civilian affairs and unwittingly creating one of the City's best known landmarks—one of the three, incidentally, that Washington would recognize if he returned today.*

Two months later the *Empress of China*, 360 tons and carrying a crew of 43, sailed past the snow-swept dunes of Sandy Hook en route to Canton by way of South Africa — the first American vessel to venture into Far Eastern waters. It would be 15 months before the *Empress* dropped anchor once more in New York Harbor, weather-beaten, but bringing to her owners a net profit of $30,727 — a satisfying 20 per cent return on invested capital. The merchants on Pearl and Water Streets began to make calculations on bits of paper and the China trade was on.

Day by day, the march of events pushed the American

---

* The other two are St. Paul's Chapel and the Jumel mansion.

Revolution deeper into the pages of history. The name of King's College was changed to Columbia. James Duane was appointed by Governor Clinton as first Mayor of New York. Washington's birthday was celebrated for the first time (February 11th instead of February 22nd), and the State Legislature petitioned Congress to return the bells of the City which had been turned over to the government at Philadelphia just before the British occupied New York.

The Continental Congress met in New York during January, 1785. Lafayette came over that summer and received the type of boisterous welcome that the City has always given to its heroes. And in the wilderness of Kentucky the grandfathers of Jefferson Davis and Abraham Lincoln struggled to clear enough land to maintain their families, unaware of the fact that within a quarter of a century their famous grandsons would be born in this same wilderness, eight months apart in time and 90 miles apart in space.

Thomas Jefferson, champion of the Common Man, was received as Minister to France by Louis XVI, champion of Aristocracy. The first hackney coach rattled over New York's cobblestones and in 1786 the first census disclosed the city's population to be 23,614, of which 2,103 were slaves.

In June of that same year General McDougall died in his Nassau Street home. His funeral was a public event, with minute-guns fired during the passage of the procession through the streets. The Bank of New York was beginning to accumulate a history.

THE NEW
CITY HALL

By 1787 the ravages of the great fire had been all but obliterated. Building was booming. Streets were being paved and extended. The old Dutch houses were beginning to disappear. At the southwest end of the island, the Hudson had been filled in for 200 feet. The trade of New Jersey, Connecticut and a large part of southern Massachusetts was flowing through New York port and New York goods were moving into the interior. The post-Revolutionary depression was all but over. New York would have setbacks in the years ahead, but nothing would ever again bring its forward movement to such a complete halt.

∘◯∘

During the hot summer of 1787 a small group of hand-picked men, meeting in Philadelphia, rendered a service to their country for which succeeding generations should be forever grateful.

The meeting was largely due to the foresight and leadership of the ever-active Hamilton who, during the previous year, had persuaded the delegates attending a convention called for the purpose of regulating inter-state commerce, that a complete overhauling of the existing machinery of government was vital to the future well-being of the nation.

The story of the Constitutional Convention and how it evolved a scheme of government, which for almost 200 years has withstood the pressures of violent and unforeseen changes, is a familiar one. The most surprising thing about it is that a group of men, chosen for their conservatism as well as their wisdom, should have taken the radical step of discarding at the outset the Articles of Confederation which they had been instructed to revise, and undertaken to re-write the Constitution from scratch. In so doing they un-questionably exceeded their authority, but they laid the sound foundations on which the Republic was to be built.

New York was the 11th state to ratify. Its Constitutional Convention met at Poughkeepsie during June, 1788, with Governor Clinton's Anti-Federalists holding a clear major-ity. Hamilton worked for delay, counting on the effect of ratification by New Hampshire and Virginia to turn the tide, and his judgment proved sound.

On July 22nd, four days before the State fell into line, a great parade was held in New York in which all trades and professions were represented. A miniature frigate, the Federal ship "Hamilton," mounting 32 guns and manned by 30 seamen was drawn down Broadway by 10 horses, its guns barking over the heads of the cheering crowds.

When news of the Poughkeepsie vote reached the City a few days later, the guns of the "Hamilton" blazed again and the bells of the churches pealed until dawn. The new Constitution was important to mercantile New York and its people seemed to sense that with its adoption the critical years were over and the United States was about to take its destined place among the free nations of the world.

THE REPUBLIC FINDS ITSELF

As the momentous year 1789 began, Major Pierre Pierce L'Enfant, engineer, architect, future designer of the Na- 1789-1800 tional Capitol at Washington, bustled nervously through the draughty rooms of the old City Hall on Wall Street, urging the workmen to greater speed so that all might be ready on March 4th for the convening of the first Congress under the new Constitution.

It was not ready but neither was the Congress.* Traveling conditions were so bad that it was April 6th before a quorum could be brought together to choose General Washington as the first President of the United States.

Spring had arrived among the rolling hills of northern Virginia when Washington left Mount Vernon for the long journey to New York. The route had become all too familiar to him during the dark days of war. Now, however, instead of being opposed by a hostile army he was greeted at every hamlet by cheering crowds. At Elizabethtown he boarded a barge manned by 13 white-uniformed "pilots." Followed by a procession of official boats, he passed across the upper bay through a lane formed by craft of every description while the guns at the Battery boomed a 13-gun salute.

Seven days later Washington took the oath of office on the balcony of the new Federal Hall while a huge crowd, jammed into the intersection of Wall and Broad Streets, and without the benefit of amplifiers, watched the ceremony in awed silence.

New York was a gay capital during the spring and summer of 1789. The Old Families had redecorated their town houses and bought splendid new liveries for their staffs of

* As late as March 24th the Common Council of the City of New York called upon The Bank of New York for a loan of £2,000 to enable the work to proceed.

negro servants; the merchants had replenished their wine cellars and the storekeepers written frantic letters to Europe ordering more merchandise.

It was a period which made up in bounteousness what it lacked in conveniences. Food was plentiful. A statement of Washington's household expenses for three months includes among the items "butcher's meat," bacon, tongue, geese, ducks, turkeys, chickens, "birds," fish, lobsters, crabs, oysters, ice cream and various kinds of fruits. The wines and liquors include madeira, claret, champagne, arrack, "spirits," brandy, cordials, porter, beer and cider.

Clothes were ostentatious and expensive for both men and women. Hairdressing was complex and constant. Extremes were the order of the day. Men as well as women affected brilliant colors. John Ramage, the miniature painter, is described as wearing a scarlet coat with mother-of-pearl buttons, a white silk "weskit" embroidered with colored flowers, black satin breeches with knee buckles, white silk stockings, large silver buckles on his shoes, and a small cocked hat on the upper part of his powdered hair, "leaving the curls at his ears displayed." John Shepherd, a tailor at 23 Hanover Square, advertised cloths of "nearly 100 different colors," including bottle green, batwing, parson's gray, changeable pearl, London smoke, mulberry, sea green, mouse's ear and drake's head.

Life was a round of balls and levees, teas and card parties, dinners prolonged by endless toasts and oratory, "promenading" and, at the slightest pretext, parades and fireworks. The John Street Theatre had recently been opened.

Washington was a frequent visitor and the playwright, Dunlap, makes the interesting note that on one such occasion "he indulged in that which was with him extremely rare, a hearty laugh."

The fashionable world stayed in town that summer, braving the heat in their freshly redecorated homes. Lodgings were at a premium. New York was crowded to bursting with statesmen, politicians, office seekers, solicitors of special privilege, and those who merely came to see the show.

At the core of all this milling about, in the remodelled City Hall, the atmosphere was far from frivolous. An immense task was being undertaken. A prodigious amount of work must be done. And the small group of men chosen for the responsibility appreciated its importance.

Their first act was to set up the essential executive departments of the new government. Thomas Jefferson was appointed Secretary of State, Hamilton, Secretary of the Treasury and Major General Knox, who only a few years before had accepted the surrender of Fort George, became Secretary of War.

In France, a mob razed the Bastille. The news was shocking, but people were too busy to grasp its full significance. In the beginning the sympathy of most Americans was with the Revolutionists, but the execution of a king was too violent a remedy for conservative sensibilities and opinion became divided. When France declared war on Great Britain, the real problem was no longer one of partisanship, but how to stay out of the conflict on either side.

As British warships continued to seize American merchant vessels, New York began to fortify Governor's Island in preparation for the worst. Patriotic fever ran high and the various trades of the City volunteered their services without much regard for their fitness. On May 7, 1793, the *Daily Advertiser* carried a notice that "the peruke makers and hairdressers of the City are to work on this day on the fortifications now erecting on Governor's Island." It was fortunate, perhaps, that the results of their efforts were never to be tested.

∘◯∘

A Federal census taken in 1790 indicates that the population of the United States had increased to almost 4,000,000. New York, with a population of 38,000 showed an increase of 70 per cent during the seven years since the Revolution and was exceeded in size only by Philadelphia.

It was still a rural nation, however. There were only five cities of any consequence, and their combined population was less than 122,000. The other 3,800,000 Americans lived on plantations, in small villages and on lonely farms, isolated by bad roads and cut off from the world by lack of newspapers and books.

The westward drift was beginning. The thud of axes heralded its slow progress through the wilderness. Along the game and Indian trails, buckskin-shirted hunters pushed ahead of the settlers. Over the crude mountain roads oxen strained at the yokes of overloaded Conestoga wagons. On the rivers, in ever-greater number, floated the rafts and the flat boats of the pioneers.

Along the seaboard, manufacturing was making a halting start. Young Sam Slater was laying the foundation of a textile empire in Rhode Island. The tinware and clocks of Connecticut were becoming popular items in the wagons of the peddlers. In the middle states a limited amount of paper and iron was being produced. New York shipyards rang with the sound of saws and hammers as the new flag of the United States was seen more and more frequently on the seas of the world.

The flow of produce and merchandise through the port of New York increased each year to the enrichment of the merchants and the consequent prosperity of The Bank of New York. After three years in its original home in the Walton House, the Bank moved into larger quarters at 11 Hanover Square. It was still operating without a charter, however, and on July 5, 1789, it renewed its application only to have it refused once more. A bill was finally framed which was passed with amendments and signed by Governor Clinton on March 21st, 1791. At long last the Bank was established as an incorporated institution with a capital of $900,000.

In the meanwhile it was not forgotten by its most interested founder, the new Secretary of the Treasury. In the early fall of 1789 it made available to the government a credit of $200,000. *Warrant No. 1* in the amount of $20,000 was drawn on the Bank on September 13th of that year—the first loan to the new Federal Government. This warrant is still in the Bank's possession. The Bank continued to make loans to the government during the early '90s.

The most important event during Washington's first term as President was the submission by Hamilton of a fiscal program to the House of Representatives which took the form of a series of reports.

In his first report Hamilton recommended funding the foreign and domestic debt at par and the assumption by the Federal Government of $20,500,000 of state debt. There was little disagreement with his proposal for handling the foreign indebtedness, but the assumption of the state debt, a large portion of which had passed into the hands of speculators, led to violent opposition, particularly from the Southern states.

The plan was finally accepted, but only after a compromise between Madison and Hamilton by which Hamilton undertook to secure enough northern votes to insure the location of the new national capitol on the Potomac, in return for which Madison agreed to produce enough southern votes to effect passage of the Assumption Bill.

Hamilton's second report dealt with an excise tax on distilled liquors, the third recommended the establishment of a national bank and the fourth proposed protective tariffs for manufacturing enterprises and other measures designed to promote industry.

Of all Hamilton's proposals, that having to do with the creation of a national bank caused the most controversy. He conceived of an institution organized along the lines of the Bank of England, designed to aid the Federal government with loans as well as in the collection of taxes and the administration of public finance. Its constitutionality was immediately challenged by the Jeffersonian group. Hamilton countered with the concept that the Constitution authorized Congress to "make all laws that shall be necessary and proper" for carrying out powers specifically granted by the Constitution and that the proposed bank fell into this category. It was the doctrine of "implied powers"—one that was to be upheld years later by Chief Justice Marshall.

Washington accepted Hamilton's argument and signed the bill creating the Bank of the United States in February, 1791. The main office was opened in Philadelphia in December and a branch office was established in New York in the spring of 1792. The presence of the new bank did not injure the business of The Bank of New York. The City and the nation were growing; there was plenty of business for both and the relationship between the two banks was cooperative from the first.

During the year 1791, United States bonds began to decline in price and Hamilton employed The Bank of New York to purchase them in small lots—the first time that any United States bank had ever supported a government bond market.

Hamilton's implicit belief in the need to develop the country's manufacturing potential led him to organize the Society for Establishing Useful Manufactures in the fall of 1791. At his request, The Bank of New York loaned the Society $45,000 during the following year.

At about this time, the Bank also established an active relationship with the State of New York, agreeing to accept deposits from the State "at not more than six per cent interest," to be returned in three months. At the same time, the State Treasurer deposited with the Bank almost $2,000,000 of United States debt certificates on which the Bank was to collect interest. Later the Bank bought these certificates from the State under an agreement by which they would be paid for over a period of years, the Bank undertaking to make loans to the State in the meantime.

The American banking system was going through its adolescent period. Operating without the guidance of precedent, the banks which were in existence in 1791 were forced to improvise and experiment. Bank credit was a new and little understood force and it would be years before they would learn how to use it to the best public advantage.

There were four banks doing business in the United States by the middle of 1791: The Bank of North America in Philadelphia (1781), The Bank of New York (1784), The Massachusetts Bank in Boston (1784) and The Bank of Maryland (1791). They stood alone, each the sole representative of banking in its respective state. By 1794, however, their number had been increased to 18 and they were beginning to coalesce into a single system which became more and more integrated as communications improved and their volume of business increased.

In spite of foreign revolutions and crises, people carried on their daily affairs as if Europe did not exist. John Jacob Astor — one of the Bank's early depositors — advertised in the *New York Daily Gazette* that he gave "cash for all kinds of furs." Eli Whitney changed the course of our history with his cotton gin. Boone's Wilderness Trail was becoming a substantial wagon road under the heavy wheels of the Conestogas. John Fitch demonstrated the first steamboat operated by a screw propeller on the hill-bordered waters of Collect Pond where New York's Criminal Courts Building now stands. Yellow fever, the City's recurrent scourge, struck again in 1795, leaving 732 dead in its path. In 1796, Washington's Farewell Address appeared in Philadelphia's *Daily American Advertiser*. Written with Hamilton's assistance, it was never delivered orally; the most famous speech, perhaps, that was never made.

The financial affairs of New York City were beginning to center on Wall Street. In March, 1796, the Bank bought the northeast corner of Wall and William Streets. The cornerstone of its new building was laid in June, 1797 and the Bank moved in during the spring of the following year. It has continued to occupy the site for 161 years.

Almost immediately, however, it became necessary to provide an alternate home. Yellow fever struck again in 1798 — this time taking a toll of 2,086 lives. The need for banking quarters outside of the City to be used during these tragically frequent epidemics became imperative. Property was purchased and a suitable building erected on what is now known as Bank Street in Greenwich Village. The precaution was timely. Another epidemic occurred the following year and the Bank moved into its out-of-town office from September until cold weather brought an end to the danger. It was forced to use the Greenwich Village office three times during the next quarter century.

It was fitting that the Bank should be established in its new quarters as the 18th Century drew to a close. A way of life was coming to an end and a new epoch was dawning. The United States was on the verge of an expansion such as the world had never before witnessed — an expansion from which it would emerge as an international power before the end of the 19th Century.

On December 14, 1799, Washington died. In less than four years Hamilton would be removed from the political arena by Aaron Burr's bullet. Through their courage, faith and tireless devotion to the public interest they had done more than any other men to build a solid foundation under the nation which they had worked so hard to create. With dramatic timing they left the stage as the curtain fell on a great act in which they had played magnificently the role allotted to them by destiny.

CHAPTER II

The Nation Builders
1800-1851

1800-1812 The year 1800 has been called the year of upheaval. The groundwork of our national structure had been laid by a small group of extraordinarily able men, unhampered by organized political parties and, in the broadest sense, accountable only to their own consciences. With no precedent to guide them, they had been obliged to operate in the realm of theory. Now the time had come to fit their political concepts into a working democracy. Thomas Jefferson, social idealist and long the opponent of Hamilton, was the man selected for the task.

At the turn of the century Jefferson's new Republican Party (not to be confused with the present Republican Party which would not come into being for another 60 years) controlled the nation. Its keynote was simplicity and the elevation of the Common Man. The formalized, courtly manners of the post-Revolutionary era were already a memory of things past. On the day of his inauguration Jefferson walked from his shabby boarding house to the new Capitol Building, accompanied by a group of friends. There he spoke in behalf of a central government of limited powers, states' rights, economy and the need to maintain "honest friendship with all nations, entangling alliances with none."

∘◯∘

After 16 years, The Bank of New York at last had a local competitor in Aaron Burr's Manhattan Company, chartered during the previous year. There were now 27 banks in operation outside of New York City, located in coastal and river towns and serving a water-borne commerce based on foreign trade.

During the next 20 years this number would grow to 300 — an unexpected development considering the fact that Jefferson's Republican Party was an avowed enemy of banks. The economic picture was changing, however. The need for credit was stronger than political philosophy. The long struggle between France and Britain would continue to disrupt our foreign trade until the inevitable climax of 1812. American business was forced to develop its own resources, creating thereby a constantly increasing demand for bank accommodation from both industry and agriculture. The gap between the banks and Jefferson's Common Man was beginning to close.

New York, although no longer either a national or a state capital, continued its rapid growth. In ever greater volume the produce and manufactures of the surrounding countryside flowed on river boats and coastal sloops through its port and into the holds of its foreign-bound ships. It had already outstripped Philadelphia and was now the largest city in the country, with a population of 60,000.

It was rapidly losing its unkempt appearance. Its streets

33

were for the most part paved with cobblestones, lighted by oil lamps and bordered by brick sidewalks. Its residential section had been crowded out of Wall Street and now extended up Broadway past St. Paul's Chapel. Its skyline was pierced by the steeples of 23 churches.

The smoke of hickory logs poured from its brick chimneys into the chilly dawn of the 19th Century. Negro chimneysweeps and men carrying cans of milk on the ends of shoulder-yokes plied their trades from house to house. The sound of hammers was in the air. Far up the East River at the eastern end of present 89th Street, Archibald Gracie, director of The Bank of New York, looked from the windows of his country house across the waters of Hell Gate and over the rolling country of the Bronx, appraising the weather before starting for his office, as future mayors would do 150 years later from the same windows.

During the period between the election of Jefferson and the War of 1812 The Bank of New York had two particularly distinguished presidents, Herman LeRoy and Matthew Clarkson. LeRoy was a merchant whose firm, LeRoy, Bayard & McEvers, was at one time the most powerful business organization in America. Matthew Clarkson, Revolutionary general, state assemblyman and senator, and an intimate friend of Hamilton, Jay and Clinton, was also a leading merchant associated with his brother in the prosperous firm of S. & L. Clarkson & Company. The office of bank president had not yet become a full-time job.

Yellow fever epidemics continued to plague the city. The Bank was forced to move to its Greenwich home in

1803 and again in 1805 and 1822. The 1805 epidemic was particularly severe, causing people to flee to Greenwich in such numbers that a tent colony was established at the corner of Greenwich Street and Broadway.

After 1800 the Bank began to experience increasing local competition. In addition to The Manhattan Company (1799), the Merchants Bank was established in 1803, the Bank of America in 1812, and the City Bank of New York (now the First National City Bank of New York) in the same year. A steadily increasing population was furnishing enough business, however, to tax the facilities of all.

○◯○

As the years passed it became more and more evident that the Jeffersonian paradise was not to be achieved, at least in the immediate future. The fabulous resources of an untouched land were too alluring to permit of Utopias. The prizes were big and the struggle for their possession was correspondingly fierce. "Thoughtful men," writes Bray Hammond, "were shocked by the harshness of the Industrial Revolution and the fierce spirit of enterprise begot from it. That spirit often merged into cupidity and chicane . . . but the good banks and the good businessmen made little noise . . . Some bankers threaded their honest, conservative way through the tumult of expansion, speculation and misbehavior . . . There was concrete evidence of honesty and conservatism in the number of banks that survived, not only the difficulties of the period, but those of all subsequent ones to the present and established the

35

striking fact of continuity in an economy of dynamics and vicissitude."*

The old order was disappearing; its leaders moving from the arena. As Alexander Hamilton died one hot July morning in 1804 at the hand of Aaron Burr, the advent of the new order was symbolized by three small boats belonging to the Lewis and Clark expedition which, on that particular day, were pushing slowly and warily up the unknown Missouri between the present states of Nebraska and Iowa.

Around the Kentucky salt licks the deer, the elk and the buffalo were disappearing. Davy Crockett, who would later die a hero's death on the battered walls of the Alamo, was engaged in establishing a legend by killing "bar" in the hills of Tennessee. On the edges of the wilderness crude little general stores were springing up where wagon tracks converged or crossed — stores that made change by chopping silver dollars into eight "bits," two of which were the equivalent of 25 cents or a "quarter." And in the more remote sections, the pack horses of the Yankee peddlers, laden with pins, needles, cloth and clocks, penetrated to the ends of the trails.

o◯o

In New York a full-fledged building boom was under way and fortunes were being made in real estate. Land that had sold for 50 dollars when The Bank of New York was founded in 1784 was now valued at 1,500 dollars. There were shops on Broadway displaying a variety of merchan-

---

* Bray Hammond, *Banks and Politics in America.* p. 177.

dise which compared favorably with the shops of London. Broadway had become the street for social promenading from eleven to three each day and although carriages were not numerous, those that existed were reported by a contemporary gossip columnist as "driven to and fro during these hours with much velocity."

The principal places of amusement were the new Park Theater, capable of holding 1,200 people, and Vauxhall and Ranelagh Gardens, elaborately planted "parks," patterned after the English Vauxhall, where one might dine against a background of music and occasional fireworks.

It was a city teeming with energy and manifold activities. Plans were under way for the construction of the present City Hall. Washington's (and Hamilton's) dream of a military academy at West Point had materialized. The Free School Society opened the first public school in the United States. Fulton's *Clermont* covered the 150 miles to Albany in 32 hours. Two years later the *Phoenix*, first steamship to venture into salt water, began regular trips between New York and Philadelphia. A new stage line made scheduled trips between New York and Albany along the east side of the Hudson River which, for a fare of 10 dollars, undertook to deliver its passengers at either destination within three days.

New York was above all, however, a maritime city, its waterfront bordered by a forest of masts and yardarms and pierced by bowsprits. Beneath them the cobbled streets were piled with bales and barrels, chests and crates containing the products of the world. Iron-wheeled carts and

PARK
THEATER

wheelbarrows and the shouts of seamen and laborers combined to create a confusion that spelled prosperity. Clerks in high hats hurried among the merchandise, checking long lists, while at the nearby Tontine Coffee House the underwriters, brokers, merchants and traders conducted their business and brought themselves up to date on the news from Europe.

THE PULL OF THE WEST

There was only one cloud in the picture — the prolonged struggle between France and Britain. The latter's 1812-1839 insistence on the right to search American ships for British subjects caused relationships between the two countries to deteriorate to a point where armed conflict became inevitable. On June 19, 1812, President Madison declared a state of war to exist and for the second and last time Englishmen and Americans were fighting.

"Mr. Madison's War" was unpopular, indecisive and, to some degree, unnecessary. On the other hand, it brought with it unforeseen benefits. It united the states in a common cause and created a national unity which might otherwise have taken years to achieve. Even more important however, by cutting off imports it forced the United States to depend largely on its own products and to develop its own manufacturing facilities.

The war was over by the end of 1814, with everything just about where it had been before the shooting started. A number of reputations had been ruined. A few had been made: that of a young naval captain named Perry; a 48-

year-old general, Andrew Jackson, who captured New Orleans two weeks after the treaty of peace had been signed; a Washington lawyer, Francis Scott Key, who, inspired by the defense of Baltimore's Fort Henry, scribbled the words of *The Star Spangled Banner* on the back of an envelope.

New York City had suffered the inconvenience and business losses of a blockade. Washington had been burned. Eighteen hundred and seventy-seven Americans had lost their lives, but not in vain, for through their sacrifice the skies had been cleared and the United States stood on the threshold of 23 years of prosperity.

But it was not our overseas trade alone which caused the great upsurge in our national development. Famine and political oppression in Europe had started a stream of immigration to the United States which increased to flood proportions during the next 40 years. Furthermore, as our internal communications improved, the seemingly limited resources of the West became more and more available to those venturesome spirits willing to pay the price of hardship and to assume the risks.

North of the Ohio River land was selling for $1.25 an acre in 80-acre lots. New states were being admitted, into which settlers were moving in increasing numbers; hardbitten farmers from New England, tired of fighting its rock-strewn soil, swarthy backwoodsmen from the South, weary of trying to eke a living from the sand, and immigrant peasants hoping that they would find in this new country a fulfillment of their dreams.

Lexington, Louisville, Knoxville and Nashville had become thriving towns. By 1820 the blue skies over Pittsburgh were already tainted with coal dust. Cincinnati, the "porkopolis" of the West, was a boom town. The frontier was approaching the Mississippi. In its vanguard roamed the hunters and trappers. On its fringes stood the crude cabins of the squatters. Following them was the first wave of settlers, a strange amalgam of the educated and the ignorant, expedientists and idealists, farmers, storekeepers, politicians, lawyers, rivermen, gamblers and those to whom home would have been a jail had they remained in the East.

They led crude and frequently dangerous lives, devoid of either manners, comforts or culture, but they paved the way for the more stable group that moved slowly westward behind *them*.

o◯o

During the war an unfamiliar hush had fallen over New York's South Street. With the coming of peace, however, a flood of foreign goods was poured into the city bringing a quick prosperity to the merchants, but eventually glutting the market. Prices plummeted and customers raced to New York to participate in what had become an international bargain sale. It brought disaster to a few, but it was important to the City none the less for it set the main currents of commerce running in its direction as they have continued to do ever since.

During these early post-war days New York merchants also succeeded in diverting to New York port cotton shipments which would otherwise have been routed directly from the Southern cotton ports to Europe. It was, perhaps, one of the greatest achievements in the history of the City. It provided New York ships with east-bound cargoes for Liverpool without which the all-important "Atlantic shuttle" could not have operated successfully. It also resulted in the South's getting most of its imports by way of New York.

Following the close of the war, a flourishing business was built up with the Caribbean. One of the leading New York houses in this trade was the previously mentioned firm of LeRoy, Bayard & Company. There were familiar names stencilled on the crates and packing cases assembled along the wharves for loading into the Caribbean-bound ships: furniture from the workshop of Duncan Phyfe, carriages by James Brewster, soap by Colgate, as well as a vast miscellany of merchandise ranging from omnibuses to umbrellas.

Within four years the sailing packets appeared, the first of the ocean liners. Up to this time merchantmen had fallen into the category of "tramps" which knocked around from port to port wherever cargoes might be had, and "regular traders" which were confined to a single sea lane. The latter carried passengers and made two trips to Europe each year, one in the spring and one in the fall. Ordinarily their sailings were delayed until their holds were full, an unsatisfactory arrangement from the passengers' point of view.

In 1818 the Black Ball Line was organized with four ships, scheduled to sail on specified days "full or not" and committed to three trips a year. One of them would be the dreaded winter voyage which, on the west-bound passage, frequently took eight storm-tossed weeks, but it meant an increase of 50 per cent in earnings on capital investment. The packets did much to insure the supremacy of New York as a port city.

∘⊂⊃∘

It has been said that the City became rich by distributing its material importations and big by retaining a large part of its human importations. Between 1819 and 1860 some 5,400,000 immigrants arrived in the United States. More than two-thirds entered at New York and a goodly portion of them went no further.

They came to America hoping to better their fortunes. The few who were aggressive and intelligent succeeded beyond their most extravagant dreams, but for the majority it merely represented a change of location without much improvement in living conditions.

They came largely from Ireland — 163,000 of them in 1851 alone — and from Germany. They also came from Italy and Austria, Poland, Spain, and Czechoslovakia. They changed the ethnic character of the city, its politics and its religions, but above all they provided a supply of unskilled labor in a pre-machinery age without which the whirlwind development of the United States would have been impossible. They built our railroads, our canals and our turnpikes, they constructed our expanding cities and they tilled the vast new acres of the West. America owes them a debt of gratitude.

43

The dominating theme of the American story, however, during the first half of the 19th Century, was the ever-accelerating westward migration, a movement only made possible by constantly improving communications.

At the close of the War of 1812 news could travel no faster than the vessels or the horses that bore it. Except in the neighborhood of the cities, movement was more or less restricted to the waterways. Roads, being either impassable most of the time or non-existent, the farmers west of the Alleghenies were forced to use the long river route to New Orleans to dispose of their produce. Coastal traffic depended on small sailing craft which had no assurance as to when they would reach their destination. There was no method of travel that did not suffer from the uncertainties of wind and weather.

Due to the work of inventors and scientists on both sides of the Atlantic, steam was being harnessed to do man's work. Its uses were restricted in the beginning, its applications crude, but within a few decades it was destined to create a world which would have been unrecognizable to the Founding Fathers.

In 1817, ten years after Fulton's *Clermont* made the trip from New York to Albany without blowing up, 120-foot steamships were plowing the waters of the Hudson, and Fulton had established a coastal line between New York and New Haven. A month before the completion of the Erie Canal in 1825 its ultimate obsolescence was foretold when the first locomotive was run over the crude rails of the Stockton and Darlington Railway in England.

It was the Erie Canal, however, rather than steam, which gave New York City its initial commercial ascendency by providing the West with direct access to the Atlantic Ocean at New York port. With its opening in October 1825, the flour, the wheat and the diversified products of western New York and Ohio literally flowed toward New York, but what was even more important to the merchants of the city, their imports could now reach the western farmers. To cement this new relationship, New York advanced money to the farmers against future crops, thus drawing interest to its banks and assuring itself of the farmers' products for export. Rival cities were never able to budge New York from the advantage which it gained in these early years, even after the railroads had overshadowed the importance of the Canal.

Roads were also beginning to connect the principal cities and in 1818 the initial section of the National Turnpike between Cumberland and Wheeling was opened. It was eventually extended to St. Louis, the first of the great toll roads. Night and day the heavy, six-horse Conestoga wagons laden with freight and settlers rumbled over its uneven surface. Droves of cattle, horses, hogs and sheep disputed the right of way with the stage coaches, powdering their passengers with choking dust. Beyond St. Louis, last outpost of civilization, transport travelled over the Santa Fé and Oregon trails which were slowly becoming defined by 'the hooves of the oxen and the iron-bound wheels of the wagons.

It was a world which had urgent need for credit and banking facilities. All through the nation banks were being chartered. Some were well managed but, unfortunately, the majority, scattered among the outlying towns and villages, were run by speculators more interested in furthering their personal schemes through the issue of bank notes than in sound banking.

New York, as the leading exporter of Southern cotton, and the products of the West, as well as the port through which passed most of the nation's imports, became the financial center of the country. Its banks multiplied, but in spite of that The Bank of New York maintained its position in the City's growing financial business.

The War of 1812 and the blockading fleets of the British had put a strain on the banks for which they were not prepared. Three months before the peace treaty was signed specie payments were suspended in New York and Philadelphia, not to be resumed until February, 1817. These were minor difficulties, however; corrective pauses in the forward movement. Over the long run the development of the nation's vast resources could result in nothing but prosperity.

It was the era of New York's merchant princes. During the next 45 years fortunes would be made — many of which are still in existence. A large number of these shrewd, aggressive men came from New England, a fact which was bitterly resented by the old Knickerbocker element in the City which felt itself, quite correctly, to have been displaced by the thin-lipped aliens from the Northeast.

THE IMMIGRANTS

The portraits of the early merchants reveal their character. These determined, unsmiling faces belong to men of integrity who could be counted upon to drive a hard bargain and who would expect both parties to live up to it, whatever the sacrifice.

In 1830 a number of the Bank's officers and directors participated in the founding of the New York Life Insurance and Trust Company with which The Bank of New York was to merge almost 100 years later. Insurance business and investment banking were frequently combined during this early period.

A post-war slump hit the City in 1819, but within a decade it had been forgotten. New York and the country at large were definitely in the midst of a boom. Accumulated money was pressing for new outlets. Inflation had set in and, in accordance with the familiar pattern it was difficult to see what was going to stop it.

In New York, prosperity was eventually brought to a halt by the great fire of 1835 which gutted a huge area south of Wall Street and destroyed over 600 buildings. The Bank of New York was spared, but by the narrowest of margins — buildings on the opposite side of Wall Street being entirely ruined by fire.

By this time it had become evident to those whose business it was to look the future in the face, that a drastic economic readjustment was in the making. All over the nation speculation had been increasing in public land and in practically every other form of tangible property from city lots to mines. By 1836 it had reached fever pitch.

Much of it was financed by means of excessive note issues on the part of the small country banks of which there were then almost 600.

To add further fuel to the inflationary flames, Congress passed an act in 1836 distributing to the states the Government's first Federal surplus in the form of "deposits" which were, in effect, grants. The growth of the nation had permitted the national debt to be paid off by 1835. Customs receipts, swollen by a huge increase in imports and land sales, exceeded expenditures to such a degree that the government found itself with a 42 million dollar surplus which was too great a temptation for the Congress.

As a final nudge toward the approaching financial debacle, President Jackson caused a "specie circular" to be issued, providing that payment for public lands must thereafter be made in hard money. Intended to protect the poor man, it actually hit him the hardest as the speculators were in a better position to lay their hands on specie.

Europe became alarmed. The Bank of England began to reject the paper of houses with large American interests. Demand for cotton fell off and its price fell with it. In May 1837, specie payment was suspended by the American banks and Britain shut off all credit.

Business came to a virtual standstill. There were bread riots in New York, in the course of which mobs sacked stores and warehouses. A nation in which only a few months before every citizen had seemed on the road to wealth, suddenly found itself in an economic quagmire to which it could find no bottom.

49

The Bank of New York remained strong during its first major crisis. It took advantage of State authorization to borrow £112,500 in London and it also borrowed approximately $300,000 from domestic sources. On the other hand, it paid its regular four per cent dividend just after the fire and in October of the same year it paid a dividend of 10 per cent.

CONTINENTAL UNITED STATES TAKES SHAPE

1839-1851   In spite of the tremendous losses caused by the panic, nothing could stop the forward surge of a burgeoning nation. During the month of April, 1838, after years of waiting for trans-Atlantic steam service, New York saw two rival trans-Atlantic steamships enter the harbor within four hours of one another. The graceful sailing packets which had done so much to build New York's mercantile prestige would remain in use for another decade, but, from the day that the little *Sirius* and the big *Great Western* steamed through the Narrows, their end was in sight.

It was a fitting incident with which to usher in the 15-year period of expansion which lay ahead, a period in which the outlines of continental United States would be filled out, the discoveries and inventions of the last two decades would be further developed and the groundwork laid for the industrial break-through which followed the Civil War. It was a period which would contain some of the most colorful episodes in our history and in its course issues would be crystallized which would come close to destroying the nation which created them.

It would not be a period distinguished for good taste, however. Pioneer life discouraged estheticism. The public favored the spectacular, the romantic and the moral.

A concert manager packed his house by advertising that 40 pianists would play simultaneously with 5 orchestras and 1,800 singers. In the field of art people sought sentimentalized landscapes depicting the pleasanter aspects of everyday life. For those who could not afford original paintings, Currier and Ives covered the walls of thousands of humble homes from Maine to California. And for those who regarded portraits in the parlor as the hallmark of gentility, but could not pay an artist's fee, a young Frenchman by the name of Daguerre invented a process which produced likenesses of anyone willing to place his head in an iron clamp for a few minutes.

In music, the nostalgic folk songs of Stephen Foster captivated the country and in rapid succession *Swanee River*, *My Old Kentucky Home* and *Old Black Joe* became imbedded in the American heart. New Yorkers seeking entertainment might take their entire family to the American museum of P. T. Barnum where, in the course of an afternoon, they could stare at General Tom Thumb, take in a Wild West show and a bathing beauty contest and listen to an educational lecture.

Barnum, however, had ambitions. He wanted to be recognized as something other than a humbug and he spent a fortune publicizing the undistinguished voice of a rather plain Swedish girl named Jenny Lind with such success that almost overnight "the Swedish Nightingale" became a national heroine whom crowds fought to hear—and Barnum became an impresario.

Out of New York harbor the canvas-laden square riggers were "rolling down to Rio," and thence around the capes of Good Hope and the Horn, bound for the Far East and the unexplored islands of the South Pacific, to return months, sometimes years, later laden with strange, romantic cargoes which enriched their owners in a single voyage.

They were cargoes of value rather than of bulk so that speed ultimately became more important than capacity. Gradually the lines of the Pacific-bound vessels grew longer and slimmer, the sail areas greater, until the china clipper evolved — the most beautiful sailing ship ever built by man.

On the flatboats of the Ohio, on the round-nosed barges of the Erie Canal, along the dusty National Turnpike, the stream of settlers moved steadily westward. In the early years they had built their homes in timbered lands along the rivers where material was readily available for cabins, fencing and firewood; and the river was their highway. "Striking out for the tall timber" they called it. Few ventured into the treeless prairies until after 1840 when they discovered that the deep virgin soil of this untouched land was black gold to the farmer.

Back in New York, James Gordon Bennett was fascinating the upper class female readers of his *New York Herald* with a "society page" while he lured the business man with a Wall Street section and the less erudite were brought into his orbit by a type of "yellow journalism" which was new to the American press. A few blocks away Horace Greeley, with his recently founded *New York Tribune*, increased his circulation by waging war on the immorality of the *Herald* and the *Sun*, championing the causes of "abolitionism, feminism, temperance and protective tariffs," and advising the youth of the City to "go west."

Down into the new Republic of Texas the settlers filtered. In clouds of choking alkaline dust they moved slowly across the desert to Mexican-owned California. Along the Santa Fé Trail creaked the lumbering "freighters," through country swarming with hostile Comanche and Kiowas. Over the 2,000 miles of the Oregon Trail crawled the canvas-covered wagons bound for the lonely abundance of the Willamette Valley.

The Republic of Texas became part of the Union in 1848. Following the Mexican War, California and the Southwest fell into place like the final pieces of a picture puzzle. Except for a few minor adjustments continental United States as we know it today had taken shape.

It was a good time to live. The air was charged with aggressiveness and vitality. Something big and powerful was being built by free men, unhampered by governmental restrictions. It was an era of opportunity in which almost anyone could find a niche only limited in depth and size by his brains and energy.

A Lowell, Massachusetts, textile mechanic invented a machine that would sew. Cyrus McCormick perfected his reaper. An artist by the name of Samuel Morse invented something called "the electro-magnetic telegraph."

Gold was discovered in California. Edgar Allan Poe, William Cullen Bryant and Nathaniel Hawthorne were creating an American literature. Charles Dickens visited America and didn't think much of it. The Croton Aqueduct at long last provided New York with an adequate water supply.

In Europe Karl Marx was distributing his *Communist Manifesto*. In the South the first Southern cotton mills were being established in North Carolina. In the West copper and iron ore were discovered in the Marquette Range and on the Oregon Trail young Francis Parkman was ruining his health as well as laying the foundations of his literary reputation.

In New York the third, and present, Trinity Church had taken its position at the head of Wall Street. The fashionable but restless residential district had moved north to Union Square. A cast iron building, precursor of the modern steel and glass skyscraper, had been erected on the corner of Washington and Murray Streets where it still stands. Wooden Indians guarded the entrances of an innovation called cigar stores. The German piano makers — Steinway, Weber, Knabe and others — were establishing their famous factories. And *Harper's Magazine* had begun its long-lived contribution to American literary history.

It did not seem that anything could interfere with a prosperity founded on natural, seemingly inexhaustible, resources and developed by people endowed with bold ingenuity and tireless energy. Only a small group of men saw the clouds that in a decade would produce a savage war.

CHAPTER III

Great Experiment Endangered
1851-1865

The sound of distant drums was in the air for the few who chose to hear.

The issue of slavery moved across the face of the land 1851-1861 like a sinister shadow. People reacted to it violently, but they likewise rejected the thought that this was something that could not be resolved by words. They were stirred to anger or approval by the fiery oratory of men like Henry Ward Beecher and William Lloyd Garrison, but ultimately the vast majority only asked to be left in peace to support their families.

But the shadow continued to lengthen and curious little eddies kicked up the dust before it. In 1852 a mother of six children wrote, in what she described as her "spare time," a book called *Uncle Tom's Cabin*. To her amazement it sold half a million copies in the United States within five years, while the people of England, who perhaps saw more clearly, being further removed from the scene, purchased a million and a half copies during the first year.

In 1854 a chunky little Senator named Douglas caused a bill to be passed creating the territories of Kansas and Nebraska and leaving the question of whether they should come into the Union slave or free, to the settlers within their borders. An angry wave of protest swept the North, in the wake of which the new anti-slavery Republican Party was born, assuming the name of Jefferson's original party with his declaration written into its platform.

And from the prairie villages of Illinois came the voice of a tall, raw-boned young lawyer who spoke against slavery in phrases of such simple, compelling clarity that they were heard across the nation.

All words as yet, but violence lay just beneath the surface, ready to erupt. In the Senate Charles Sumner, outspoken free-soiler and one of the founders of the new Republican Party, was brutally beaten by Representative Preston Brooks of South Carolina. In Boston, an angry mob, coming to the rescue of a captured runaway slave, had to be dispersed by troops. At Harper's Ferry a half-crazed old man from Kansas ended his erratic career in a Valkyrian finale and caused his battered body to be immortalized in a Civil War marching song.

In New York, the merchants and the bankers wore anxious expressions. The City had become the distributing center for European textile imports and the South was one of its biggest customers. Even more important, Southern cotton was New York's most valuable export. Many of the Southern planters were heavily in debt to the merchants and bankers for crops that were still in the ground and for goods purchased. Small wonder that the mention of disunion caused the latter's foreheads to grow uncomfortably damp.

The attention of most business men was so concentrated on the widening rift between the North and South that they failed to note the approach of trouble from another quarter.

The United States had again been over-betting on its own future. Speculation had out-stripped the realities of life in railroad building, mining, real estate, and almost every other phase of the country's development. California gold was arriving in the East in such quantities that it was depreciating. The consequence was a rise in prices which acted as a booster rocket to an already over-expanded economy. Credit increased, maturities lengthened. Once again the man in the street envisioned the millenium as lying just ahead.

On August 8th, 1857, the failure of the Ohio Life Insurance & Trust Company touched off a panic. Money rates soared to a peak of 5 per cent *per month*. There being no central bank to act as a lender of last resort, the banks were obliged to close down on their customers to save themselves. Specie payment was discontinued in New York on October 13th although resumed within two months. It was a short-lived panic from that point of view, but its casualties were heavy and its effects were felt for many months. In New York, almost 40,000 men were idle. "Hunger meetings" were held and the unemployed paraded through the streets demanding bread and work. The City Fathers voted $250,000 to create jobs in Central Park, which was just being laid out — the first recorded example of "made work."

By 1860, prosperity had returned once more. The South produced the biggest cotton crop in years, filling the warehouses of New England and Great Britain and in so doing, upsetting the war calculations of some of the most astute Southern leaders.

With the announcement of Lincoln's election in the fall of that year, however, the fat was in the fire. Before he took office seven states had left the Union. A month later a shot from a Charleston shore battery screamed across the bay and thudded into the thick masonry of Fort Sumter, shattering, in many cases forever, the cherished daily routines of eight million families.

o◯o

During these anxious years important things were happening to The Bank of New York which had no connection with the impending crisis.

One had to do with the creation of the New York Clearing House. As far back as 1841, Albert Gallatin, Thomas Jefferson's able Secretary of the Treasury, had advocated a more efficient method of adjusting the balances between the New York banks. No action was taken and in the meantime, the number of banks had increased to 60. Settlements were made weekly in gold which meant that 60 clerks were scuttling about the City at the same time, collecting specie here and paying it out there.

Corrective action was taken in the summer of 1853 when the New York Clearing House was organized. The Bank of New York, as the oldest institution in the City, became Number One on the list of members and its original

58

Clearing House number still appears on all of its checks.

The charter of the Bank expired in January of the same year. Under the Free Banking Act of 1838, it was entitled to go under the general banking laws of the State and to increase its capitalization. It did both, increasing its capital from $1,000,000 to $2,000,000 and at the same time changing its official name from "The President, Directors and Company of The Bank of New York" to "The Bank of New York" — its present title.

The Bank had occupied its offices on the corner of Wall and William Streets for 57 years. Its business had expanded with the growth of the City and the Nation. Larger quarters had become imperative. On September 10, 1856, the cornerstone of a new building was laid on the old site. It was completed in 1858. Among its first tenants was the New York Clearing House which remained with it until 1874.

○◯○

While the shadow lengthened, America's creative energy continued unchecked. Much of it was directed to the conquest of distance and terrain, spurred on by the westward movement which never ceased despite war or economic crises.

By 1855 New York was joined to Chicago by a continuous line of rails and by 1860 they extended as far west as St. Joseph, Missouri. Stagecoaches linked the Mississippi River and the Pacific Ocean for those willing to risk Indian attacks and the guns of road agents, while the Pony Express riders, soon to be eliminated by the telegraph lines, staged

US MAIL
PACKET
NATCHEZ

1855~60

their last great show by carrying Lincoln's *Inaugural Address* from "St. Joe" to the West Coast in the remarkable time of seven days and 17 hours.

As industrial growth swept over New England and the Middle States, the cities kept pace with it. In 1790 there had been only six cities with a population of over 8,000; when Lincoln was elected 70 years later there were 141, and in this brief span the national population had risen from approximately 4,000,000 to 31,500,000.

The minutiae of daily life continued to fill the columns of the newspapers. The New York-built yacht, *America*, won the International Regatta at Cowes, returning with a homely trophy since proudly referred to as the "America's Cup." A group of Greeley associates, preferring journalism to reform, founded *The New York Times*. In Bryant Park a huge glass and iron monstrosity known as the "Crystal Palace" was erected for America's first World's Fair. In Brooklyn a bearded newspaper editor wrote *Leaves of Grass*.

An English sport called "croquet" was rolling over the close-clipped lawns of Long Island and a card game called "poker" had given a new significance to Saturday night. Everyone was talking about a book titled *Origin of Species* in which a daring Englishman had had the audacity to link men with monkeys. Joseph Jefferson was captivating audiences with Rip Van Winkle. A passenger elevator operated by steam was being installed in the new Fifth Avenue Hotel.

Then, suddenly, the thunder of Horace Greeley's oratory, the whir of the textile looms, the non-stop arguments in the salons and saloons, the rattle of drays over cobbles, the chunking of the paddlewheels on the Mississippi River, the rumble of trains, all the sounds that merge to become the voice of a nation, were drowned by the dull booming of the guns and an odd hush fell over an incredulous land.

STORM OVER AMERICA

Great wars almost inevitably bring about drastic and permanent changes in the economic and social life of a country. Once committed to arms, belligerents seldom regain their pre-war status. The demands of the Civil War were directly responsible for the culmination of the American industrial revolution, causing the greatest forward surge in technical achievement that the world had seen up to that time and laying the groundwork for the rise of big business in the post-war decades.

1861-1865

The more immediate effect of the war was to precipitate a severe, though short-lived, panic in the North. The apprehension of the New York merchants had been well founded. When the war began, Southern interests owed the banks and business establishments of the North close to $300,000,000 — practically all of which was a total loss.

In spite of this staggering write-off, the following spring saw a revival of prosperity resulting from the insatiable needs of a rapidly expanding army. Manufacturing, protected by an increasing tariff, responded to the crisis by producing on a hitherto·unprecedented scale, and the Homestead Act of 1862, which granted 150 acres of land free to almost anyone who would live on them for five years, brought a new flood of immigration to the United States with a consequent increase in vitally needed agricultural production.

New York was, of course, never in serious danger of attack although there were recurrent apprehensions, particularly after the *Merrimac* destroyed three Federal frigates off Newport News in the second year of the war. The City's most serious disturbance occurred during July, 1863, as a result of the first Federal draft, then in progress. The Conscription Act provided that draftees could avoid service by payment of $300 or by producing a substitute. This was understandably regarded as being inequitable to the poor. Mobs destroyed many of the recruiting centers, sacked the offices of Greeley's *Tribune,* and attacked and lynched negroes who were held to be the cause of the war. The Colored Orphan Asylum, which stood just south of the present Fifth Avenue Bank Office of The Bank of New York, was attacked and burned. Rioting was put down after four days by troops hurried east from the battle-fields of Gettysburg.

Financing the war presented a more difficult problem for the government than supplying its material needs. The national fiscal machinery was totally inadequate to meet the demands of a major conflict. Salmon P. Chase, Secretary of the Treasury, was a lawyer suddenly called upon to be a financier and he found the transition a difficult one. Fortunately, the New York banks had taken precautionary measures. In November, 1860, five months before the war

63

began, they had pooled their specie resources, each bank holding Clearing House certificates for the amount of its share.

In August, 1861, Secretary Chase came to New York and met with the banks of New York, Philadelphia and Boston. A loan was arranged in the amount of $150,000,000 secured by bonds which the banks might resell to the public. To the surprise of the banks, however, which had supposed that the loan would be made in the form of book credits, the Secretary demanded specie because of his interpretation of existing law. This required far more gold than the banks possessed, with the result that the loan had to be made in three installments and even then it depleted dangerously the banks' gold reserves.

Secretary Chase had reasoned that the gold would be paid out by the Treasury in discharge of its obligations and would then flow back to the banks. Much of it did not, however, and the shortage of specie grew increasingly acute as hoarding became more prevalent. Specie payment was suspended by the banks in December, 1861, and the government immediately followed suit.

It soon became obvious that the notes of the state banks could not meet the demand for a circulating medium. Early in 1862, Congress authorized its first government note issue in an amount which, with subsequent increases, eventually reached $450,000,000.

These were the famous "greenbacks." Following the principal of Gresham's Law that cheap money drives out the stronger currency, hard money all but disappeared from circulation. The "greenbacks" depreciated and prices soared during the next three years. Wages also rose, but not to the same degree, involving much hardship on the lower income groups.

In 1862 the paper money of 1,600 state banks was circulating at varying discounts. In view of the fact that there was no practical way of evaluating the strength of most of the issuing banks, the resulting situation was obviously chaotic. To eliminate this condition a national banking system was established under the National Banking Act of 1863.

The objective of the Act was to bring the banks under Federal control. Existing banks might take out Federal charters at which time they would deposit with the Treasury government bonds equal to one-third of their capital, against which they might issue notes up to 90 per cent of the market value of the bonds.

Although this action was voluntary, it had been expected that a majority of the existing banks would surrender their state charters and go into the national system. This did not prove to be the case. The New York banks, in the beginning at least, opposed the Act, preferring to weather the storm under their present system and retain their independence. They also objected to a clause in the Act requiring complying banks to drop their old names and assume numbers. To the 80-year-old Bank of New York this was particularly undesirable.

This arbitrary and meaningless requirement was eventually eliminated and on July 16, 1865, The Bank of New

York became a national bank under the title of "Bank of New York N. B. A." It had stood up well during the war years. Its business and its dividends had increased. The latter had risen from three per cent in 1861 to five per cent in December 1863, and had remained at that level until the close of the war.

On April 4, 1865, Lee's armies surrendered at Appomattox. The United States, matured by common suffering, surveyed the wreckage and faced the future uncertainly, little knowing that it stood on the threshold of an industrial and business expansion which, in little more than half a century, would make it the richest and strongest nation in the world.

CHAPTER IV

Emergence of Modern America
1865-1914

The aftermath of war tends to follow a pattern: in the beginning an insatiable demand for products long denied resulting in abnormal activity, rising prices, the emergence of new political and business leaders, increasing speculation, over-production and the final phase of economic collapse. 1865-1877

The post-war cycle from 1865 to 1877 followed this formula. The change in national leadership came with tragic suddenness on the heels of Appomattox. Lincoln's well-meaning, but inept successor, Andrew Johnson, quickly lost control of the situation. As the reins slipped from his fumbling fingers, they were seized by men who sought to punish and exploit rather than to heal the wounds left by the war.

Into the exhausted and shattered South poured a hostile motley of Federal troops, Northern politicians and self-seekers, beginning a sordid chapter in our national history which would only terminate twelve years later when President Hayes recalled the troops and brought "reconstruction" to an unmourned end.

In the North, inflation was in full swing. A new crop of millionaires had been raised by the war, to many of whom the responsibility of wealth was less important than its acquisition. It was an unhealthy philosophy, but one which eventually permeated the thinking of an entire generation and opened the doors to political robbers like Boss Tweed and his "ring" and to stock manipulators like Daniel Drew, Jay Gould and "Jubilee Jim" Fisk.

In the West steel rails were being laid across the prairies and the deserts at a speed which seemed incredible to the Old Timers. The white-topped prairie schooners were being replaced by funnel-stacked locomotives which threw plumes of black smoke into the dry desert air. More than 30,000 miles of track were laid between 1865 and 1873. Natural resources, which had been practically inaccessible before the war, were now, for the first time, within reach of those with the courage to seize and the strength to hold.

Gold was discovered in the Black Hills in 1875, introducing the last act in the picturesque drama of the Old West. The actors in this colorful finale have become a part of American folklore; Wild Bill Hickok, the straight-shooting Federal marshal with the lightning draw, Calamity Jane, Buffalo Bill and twisted characters like Jesse James and Billy the Kid, prototypes of the trigger-happy badman.

o◯o

New York, with its financial contacts, was the first to feel the stir of post-war activity in the form of a major building boom. In 1865 it was a "low" city of three- and four-story houses, its skyline pierced by the steeples of churches and occasionally broken by a six-story building which towered above its neighbors.

It terminated abruptly at 57th Street and the journey to the northern end of the Island was a long and inconvenient one. Actually it was easier for a New York business man, with an office in the downtown section, to live in the suburbs of Long Island, Staten Island or New Jersey rather than to attempt the daily trip from and to the northern end of Manhattan.

The City was growing faster than its facilities. In 1866 Dr. Samuel Osgood in an address before the New York Historical Society made some comments which have a familiar ring to modern ears. "New York," he said, "is like an overgrown boy whose clothes are too small for his limbs and who waits in half-nakedness for his fitting garments. The scarcity of houses and the cost of rent, living and taxation are . . . driving a large portion of our middling class into the country."

○◯○

The year 1865 marks the threshold of the familiar. The old, hand-drawn fire engines were replaced by the horse-drawn type that was to quicken the hearts of small boys for generations to come.

New Yorkers, always on the alert for opportunities to crowd into smaller quarters, were beginning to live in what were currently known as "French flats," the progenitors of the modern apartment house.

The first experimental half mile of elevated railway (cable driven) appeared on Greenwich Street. Stock tickers were introduced, indicating the growing importance of the Stock Exchange. Quantities of long-haired buffalo robes were beginning to enfold the knees of Eastern sleigh riders as the great slaughter on the western plains gathered momentum.

The new crop of millionaires, uncertain as to whether their success was fully appreciated, sought to establish their identity once and for all by building castles and chateaux. In the night spots of laughter-loving, amoral New Orleans an odd musical rhythm was incubating which would later be called Jazz. Foresighted George N. Pullman built the first especially constructed sleeping car which resulted in the organization of the Pullman Palace Car Co.

Across the plains, moving simultaneously from the west and from the east, the rails of the Union Pacific came together at a snail's pace. Under the fierce sun, Irish, Germans, Mexicans, Chinese and a generous sprinkling of ex-convicts worked side by side, grading, laying the heavy rails and driving the spikes that held them in place, with one eye constantly on their stacked rifles in readiness for a sudden Indian attack — all for $2.50 a day.

Fifteen months after Appomattox that costly white elephant the *Great Eastern* laid the first successful Atlantic cable, linking two continents. On May 10, 1869, the steel lines of the Union Pacific met at Promontory, Utah and the two seas were also linked for the first time. Six months later the Suez Canal was opened. Man's world was shrinking and as it grew smaller its tempo increased. Within a decade the telephone would shatter the privacy of the home and the clatter of typewriters would signal the end of legible handwriting and leisurely personal correspondence.

Old landmarks were disappearing. New ones were taking their place. On 42nd Street the first Grand Central Station was opened in 1871. The following year the Presbyterian Hospital moved into new quarters on 70th Street between Madison Avenue and Park. The American Museum of Natural History occupied the first building on its present site in 1877 and in 1875 The Fifth Avenue Bank, which 73 years later would merge with The Bank of New York, opened its first banking offices in the old Sherwood House on the northeast corner of Fifth Avenue and 44th Street.

The population of the City had passed the million mark. New York had indeed "grown out of its clothes." Its wharves were small and unsheltered, its streets badly paved and congested, its lower income housing facilities scarcely worthy of the name and its public transportation so inadequate that most people spent a considerable part of each day struggling to get to work and then fighting to get home again — just as they do today.

An even more important result of this rapid growth was the taking over of the city government by professional politicians under whose unaltruistic guidance City Hall became a place for personal enrichment rather than for municipal government. As the average citizen became more and more occupied with his personal affairs, the standards of political morality were permitted to decline unnoticed.

During the Civil War, Tammany boss William Marcy Tweed and his so called "ring" secured control of the city's executive machinery and systematically milked the municipal treasury for almost a decade. The extent of this dairying operation has never been determined exactly, but the best estimates are that it ranged between $100,000,000 and $200,000,000.

The ring was exposed in 1870, largely through the efforts of the *New York Times* and the work of the brilliant young cartoonist, Thomas Nast, whose adaptation of the tiger to represent Tammany Hall became a fixed symbol for that organization as did his elephant and donkey for the Republican and the Democratic parties.

Tweed was arrested and convicted during the fall of 1872 and the frustrated citizens of New York breathed a sigh of relief with the exception of a small group which departed permanently for Europe.

Before the City could clear away the financial rubble left by the Tweed ring, the final phase of the post-war cycle broke over the country. The panic of 1873 was not entirely unexpected. The records indicate that at The Bank of New York it had been foreseen by President Leverich and his associates and that definite precautionary steps had been taken. It should not have been too difficult to foresee as it was the almost inevitable result of the reckless years which had preceded it. In the manner of all panics, however, it took the nation as a whole completely by surprise.

There is usually a villain in these crises and in this case it was the railroads. Since the end of the war railroad building had been proceeding without much regard to need or to the financial strains involved. Rails had been laid into regions where there could be little hope of immediate profit

73

to the stockholders and at costs which assured disproportionate profits for the builders. All too many of those responsible for the development of the railroads regarded them as a source of personal gain rather than as a public responsibility. In May, 1873, it was found impossible to place an issue of rail bonds in the European market: the red light indicating trouble ahead.

Early in the following September the wheat crop caused the usual drain on New York's funds. The thread was stretched to the breaking point and ready to snap. The failure of Jay Cooke & Company, a firm which had been considered impregnable, was the direct cause of its breaking. Numerous Stock Exchange houses failed and runs began on a number of banks. The New York Stock Exchange was closed immediately.

Once again The Bank of New York weathered a major panic without too much difficulty. In fact, its books indicate that it came out of it even stronger than it went in. Its foreign business had been increasing rapidly since cable service to Europe had become available and under President Leverich it had developed an important Southern business, both of which activities continued to grow in the decades following the panic.

Like that of 1857 it was a short crisis, but a severe one. Its casualty lists were long and its effects were felt until 1877 by which time sufficient capital had accumulated to launch the great forward movement which marked the last quarter of the century.

The post-war cycle was over. Reconstruction had ended

in the South. The Panic of 1873 had cleared the national atmosphere like an electric storm. The United States was conditioned for the most spectacular 35 years in its economic history.

RISE OF BIG BUSINESS

The story of the last years of the 19th century might well be told through its inventions, many of which would 1877-1890 eventually reduce distances and eliminate labor to an extent hitherto undreamed. In theory they would simplify man's daily life enormously although in actuality they would end by making it unbelievably complicated. In any event they would change it beyond recognition.

For the most part these early inventions were but stumbling approaches to the streamlined, incomprehensible gadgets which presently whisk us about the world or whose tangled wires clutter the baseboards of our modern homes.

The first crude phonograph was patented by Edison in 1878. In Germany and France men like Otto, Benz, Daimler and Levassor were making great strides in the development of gasolene-propelled vehicles although another ten years would elapse before the Duryea Motor Wagon Company would sell the first "horseless carriage" in America. In the Eighties the revolutionary reaper-thresher, drawn by from 20 to 40 horses, first appeared in the horizon-bounded wheat fields of the Dakotas. And a youthful inventor by the name of George Eastman patented the first roll film as a result of which he was able to place the "Kodak" between the eager hands of the American public.

The vast land areas of the United States had been largely explored. Its most critical war had been fought and the resulting fractures were healing. With the youthful energy and enthusiasm which had characterized each successive phase of its history, the people of the United States now turned to business expansion and the development of the country's natural resources.

From coast to coast the economic climate was favorable. Even in the South the sun was beginning to shine once more. By 1878 the cotton crop was back to pre-war standards and down in Durham, North Carolina, an aggressive young man by the name of James B. Duke was developing a bright leaf smoking tobacco and was also engaged in selling the United States on the virtues of cigarettes, which the Old Timers still regarded as effete.

In Pennsylvania, West Virginia, Ohio and Kentucky men were drilling for oil, a difficult, risk-laden venture which lent itself to the control of a few strong groups. By 1879 the Standard Oil Company of Ohio, representing the merged interests of Rockefeller, Harkness and Flagler, accounted for more than 90 per cent of the total oil refined each year. Steel output, stimulated by the energy of a Scotch immigrant named Carnegie, was establishing new annual records. The advantages of bigness were beginning to be felt.

The Northwest was finally opened with the completion of the Northern Pacific in 1883. In Montana, Marcus Daly, an Irish immigrant, purchased the Anaconda Silver Mine on a lucky hunch that its wealth lay in red metal rather than grey. In the Nevada Desert the Comstock Lode was creating new millionaires and in Comstock's Virginia City, unique among mining towns, the music of Wagner and Verdi drifted across the barren hills from the new opera house, while a few blocks away in the offices of the "Territorial Enterprise" a young newspaper man who signed himself "Mark Twain" scribbled out his afternoon assignment on sheets of yellow paper.

In the more orderly, but equally aggressive, atmosphere of Manhattan, The Bank of New York was celebrating its 100th birthday during a trying year. Early in February, 1884, there had commenced a steady drain of gold to Europe. By the end of April, almost $30,000,000 had been shipped out. Europe was selling American securities. Foreign exchange was moving adversely, and silver was piling up in the Treasury due to mandatory purchases.

In May the country was shocked by the suspension of General Grant's banking firm, Grant and Ward. Immediately after, two banks and five important financial houses closed their doors. New York's financial "crash program," however, had been developing over the years into a smoothly functioning machine and vigorous steps were taken promptly to extinguish the blaze.

The Bank of New York notified its customers that it had money to lend and in one hour put out over $4,000,000, a large amount for those days. A New York newspaper, commenting on this incident, said, "It is pretty well known that, but for the prompt action on the part of the Bank the Stock Exchange would have had to close."

New York was in its usual process of outgrowing itself. In appearance it was still a flat, rather drab city. Its larger buildings belonged for the most part to the "massive mansard" school with arched windows and ornate cornices, and its brownstone dwellings lined the residential streets with grim, undeviating uniformity.

Behind their chocolate-colored facades the visitor found himself in a jungle of heavy drapes and heavier furniture. It was the fringe age in interior decoration. The bottoms of the button-studded, upholstered chairs and sofas were fringed to the floor. Fringes decorated the edges of the massive curtains and hung from the multitude of scarves which draped mantles, pianos and easels. Even the ladies were beginning to fringe their hair.

Clutter was the keynote. Every available foot of floor space was filled with chairs, couches and ottomans. Bric-a-brac cluttered the mantles and the corner "whatnots." The "drawing room" walls were hidden with oil paintings and in every corner and niche, flanking every door, a pedestal was almost sure to be supporting a vase or a statue — a hazardous setting for visiting grandchildren.

It was a world of wall-to-wall carpeting, furniture whose designers seemed motivated solely by the desire to produce something that had never been seen before and, God willing, never would be again — a world of velvet, plush, huge bedsteads, antimacassars, armoires and insufficient lighting.

It was also a world of confusing contrasts, this so-called Age of Elegance, in which men in full dress and opera cloaks rubbed shoulders without embarrassment with poverty and the picturesque hangers-on of Broadway, and chic ladies unheedingly swept the dusty pavements with their long, elaborately ruffled skirts. Hansom cabs and stylish broughams threaded their way through dray-congested streets which were further blocked with "El" construction and piles of building bricks. Horse cars crawled through the confusion, so small that the impact of a heavy passenger stepping onto the rear platform could be felt by all the other occupants. Democracy had not yet become a fetish .and there were special horse cars with upholstered chairs and movable tables, operating on a fixed schedule in the morning and evening for the benefit of well-to-do commuters between midtown and Wall Street.

Bordering each side of the business streets, tall poles reached to the fourth stories of the buildings, carrying an incredible skein of wires which laced back and forth above the traffic in a seemingly hopeless tangle. The one good deed of the Blizzard of '88 was to pull them down, crippling the city for days to be sure, but ultimately causing all wires to be buried.

It was a conventional world in which women donned, for public bathing, clothing very similar to that which they wore about town except that the skirts were shorter — a reluctant concession to the desire not to drown. Men played "lawn tennis" wearing long trousers, shirts with detachable stiff collars and cuffs and either a straw "boater" or a derby, while their fair partners, who were not expected to do very much except squeal, appeared in ankle-length skirts with occasional bustles and elaborate bonnets.

The first roller-coaster appeared at Coney Island in 1884 — a lethal contraption in which the victims sat back to back, facing out, with nothing much to hang onto but their hats. Bicycle Clubs took weekend trips on high wheelers and tandems into the back country around Yonkers and New Rochelle. People said "ta-ta" on parting instead of "goodbye now" (which was, if anything, an improvement). A few wags had started the custom of tossing ticker tape from the windows of the Stock Exchange and each year Mrs. William Astor, with the assistance of that tireless social arbiter, Ward McAllister, gave a ball in the art gallery of her Fifth Avenue home. Jammed to capacity it held 400 people, from which stemmed the legend of New York's "Four Hundred."

It was a world that was conscious of elegance and quick to acknowledge its presence. We live today in an air-conditioned super-world of such chrome-studded magnificence that we would scarcely break our hurried stride to notice walls of burnished gold. In the last quarter of the 19th Century, however, the rapidly increasing tempo of progress had not yet satiated public appreciation.

When The Fifth Avenue Bank of New York opened its first banking quarters in the Sherwood House, the *Evening Post* commented, "The . . . offices are very neat and attractive . . . On the right of the entrance, which is but a step below the level of the sidewalk, are the desks of the President and Cashier and an open reception room handsomely furnished and carpeted. Among the depositors are many ladies and for *their* accommodation a parlor has been fitted

THE
5TH AVENUE
BANK

up . . . which is richly carpeted and elegantly furnished and in every way comfortable and convenient." Carpeting appears to have been city desk news in those days.

o◯o

The sudden shift of emphasis from the farm to the factory after the Civil War, spelled the ultimate doom of rugged individualism and the beginning of highly organized business enterprises. A new type of leader was emerging. During the next 40 years "captains of industry" would be the national heroes rather than statesmen, explorers or warriors. Mass production was beginning to displace the handicraftsmen, who had been the producers since the beginning of civilization. Quantity was to be emphasized henceforward rather than quality. Credit and capital would become more liquid and transferrable and the financier was due to assume an increasing importance in the American business picture.

Until the Civil War the great private fortunes had belonged to the landowners and the merchants. Now the mantle of wealth was about to be transferred to the shoulders of the industrialists and the private bankers. New names were appearing in the top brackets of the national "Who's Who" — Vanderbilt, Carnegie, Morgan, Rockefeller, Duke, Frick, Schiff, Swift, Havemeyer and a dozen others.

The spirit of bigness was in the air, fostered by the Jeffersonian doctrine that it was not the function of government to interfere with business. We have become so indoctrinated with the opposite philosophy during the last

82

quarter century that the traditional *laissez faire* attitude of the American government from Washington to Franklin D. Roosevelt is sometimes difficult to grasp. To the modern ear the phrase implies a criticism. It should not be forgotten, however, that without this *laissez faire* attitude on the part of government the United States could not have developed the industrial strength and versatility, the self-confidence and know-how, which brought it victorious through two great wars.

THE '90s — GAY AND NOT SO GAY

They called it the Gay Nineties, this final decade of a great century. The United States had reason to be gay. It 1890-1900 was strong, it was youthful and it was rich.

The wealth of the country was concentrated. The Great Leveling was decades away. Gentlemen were still recognized as such and could wear their silk hats to the hot spots without fear of having them knocked over their eyes. The young bloods still drank champagne (on occasion) out of ladies' slippers, which fashion had not yet made self-bailing. And down at the old Waldorf heavy-lidded men, the majority of whom would never hear of an income tax, watched the promenaders in Peacock Alley through the fragrant smoke of clear Havanas.

It would be a mistake to think, however, that gaiety in the '90s was undiluted. There were forces at work which were anything but gay — powerful forces which foretold, if one had the skill to read them, the social upheaval that lay ahead.

For one thing the frontier, with its color and dramatic quality, had all but passed from the American picture. Nothing quite like the Old West had ever been seen before. Probably nothing quite like it will ever be seen again. The railroads, however, with little regard for either color or drama, had made it possible for the farmers to move into the Great Plains. It was as simple as that. Gone the huge buffalo herds, gone the fierce tribes of nomadic Indians, gone the open range and the uninhibited Remington cowboy, gone the rowdy mining towns with their bawdy saloons and diamond-studded gamblers. And with them went the recklessness and the freedom of a life which has had increasing appeal ever since to the small boy which lurks in every not-so-free American male.

There were still cattle on the ranges, but they grazed prosaically within barbed wire boundaries. In the mountains mining was still a major industry, but the engineer had replaced the bush-bearded placer miner. Organized business had taken up a task which had become too big for individuals, however picturesque.

The rapid increase of urban population was another factor destined to change national thinking and habits. When The Bank of New York was founded 95 per cent of the population lived in communities of less than 2,500 people. By the beginning of the 20th century this proportion had decreased to approximately 60 per cent and the trend was rapidly acquiring momentum.

The increasing size of business units was perhaps the most important factor of all. The desirability of bringing competing firms together in order to eliminate price wars and to reduce costs was becoming increasingly obvious. The corporation had already largely taken the place of the firm and now a new instrument, known as the trust, had been devised for promoting still greater concentrations of similar business interests.

It is difficult for most of us to realize that 60 years ago trusts were a recognized form of industrial organization. A trust in 1890 was merely a combination of independent enterprises under the terms of which the stockholders of each placed their holdings in the hands of trustees who managed the business for all. Once the pattern had been established they multiplied rapidly. There was an oil trust, a lead trust, trusts for whisky, sugar, matches, tobacco and a dozen other industries.

The American people, however, have traditionally looked askance at bigness and, although they recognized the justification of larger industrial units, they feared the giant combinations which seemed to be concentrating the economic control of the nation into a small section of the Northeast. Size meant strength, but the voters feared strength in this form. Faced with a dilemma, Congress, somewhat unwillingly, passed the Sherman Anti-Trust Act of 1890, the impact of which would not be felt until Theodore Roosevelt became president in 1901.

∘◯∘

A reaction from the speculative years preceding 1890 was inevitable, and a number of events conspired to blow it up into a full-fledged, financial panic. The suspension of

Baring Brothers in 1890 caused liquidation in England which resulted in a heavy drain on our gold reserves. Speculation in railroad building had once more undermined a number of supposedly sound organizations. Cleveland's election in 1892 presaged a lowered tariff. The Democratic party was strongly inflationary and, finally, there was doubt whether the gold standard could be maintained.

In 1893 the storm broke. In that year 600 business institutions failed and 74 railroads, representing 30,000 miles of track, went into the hands of receivers. By the end of 1894 the number of bankrupt railroads had increased to 194. Unemployment and industrial unrest plagued the nation. In Chicago a strike against the Pullman Company reached such a pitch of violence that Federal troops were called upon to bring the situation under control and during the winter of 1893-94 a motley group of jobless men, known as Coxey's Army, converged on Washington to present their grievances.

∘◯∘

Financial upheaval could not crush the exuberance of this closing decade of a great century. Without fully realizing it, the United States was about to become a world power. The Hawaiian Islands went under the American flag in 1898 and in that same year the misrule of Spain in Cuba led to the Spanish-American war at the end of which the United States found itself with Puerto Rico and the Philippines on its hands — without knowing quite what to do with them.

Our memory of this shortest of wars is of Admiral

Dewey destroying an outranged Spanish fleet at Manila Bay, of the ebullient T.R. waving his campaign Stetson at San Juan Hill, of the "white squadron" rounding the Horn and Captain Hobson plugging the entrance to Santiago Bay with the *Merrimac*. At another and less spectacular level, however, the war performed a vital service to the nation by exposing the bungling inefficiency of our defense departments. The lessons learned in 1898 were invaluable in helping us to prepare for the struggle of 1918.

In 1890 the Fifth Avenue Bank moved across the avenue to the northwest corner of Fifth Avenue and 44th Street which site The Bank of New York occupies today.

Since 1870 the social life of New York had centered around Madison Square. Fifth Avenue immediately above 42nd Street was impeccably respectable, but the names that made the news were still located below the Reservoir. When, in the mid-Nineties, however, the Astors, John and William, tore down their residences to build the first Waldorf-Astoria, the *haute monde* took its cue and quietly began its northward trek.

The modest brownstones, with their rigidly aligned stoops, gave way to more pretentious dwellings. The day of the Kings was dawning on Fifth Avenue — copper kings, steel kings, cotton kings, tin kings, each of whom would build a palace suitable for the entertainment of fellow royalty, and designed to reduce all comers to a proper state of envy.

It was a brash world of white ties and brown derbies, Gibson girls and girls who had never heard of Gibson, a world of rather tasteless elegance, housed in beautiful exteriors, a comfortable, somewhat naughty world, but above all a secure world which felt that it had reached a moment in time that would never change.

TURN OF A CENTURY

1900-1914 The streets were jammed with horn-blowing revelers on New Year's Eve, 1899. A cold, raw wind foretold snow, but no one cared, for in a short while a new century was about to be born. The last few years of the outgoing century had brought such amazing changes into everyone's life that people were justified in believing that the 1900's would bring even greater surprises. They did.

The excited, noisy crowd that milled through the streets that night, almost 60 years ago, considered that it belonged to an ultra-modern world. It would have been hard to convince these people that actually they were living through the last days of a comfortable, traditional era which was about to be fragmented so completely by war, inflation, social revolution, taxes, inventions and discoveries that in 50 years it would be difficult to visualize what the world had looked like on New Year's Eve, 1899.

Three things stand out as one rereads the story of the period immediately preceding World War I: the development of the automobile; the emergence of huge national corporations; and the reform movement touched off by Theodore Roosevelt.

At the turn of the century there were only 13,824 automobiles registered in the entire United States. The horse

88

was still the basis of transportation and there was no reason to suppose that he would ever be supplanted by these costly new toys which were forever breaking down in the middle of country roads. The tempo of life was geared to the leisurely "clop-clop" of horses' hooves and there was no desire to change it.

Journeys which we now think of in terms of minutes took a day to plan and another to make. Those who worked in the cities either lived within their limits or in suburban towns, strung like beads along radiating railroad lines. In the latter event they lived within walking distance of the station unless they had the means to afford a horse and a coachman. Where the city and the suburban towns ended abrubtly, the countryside, laced by narrow dirt roads, looked just about as it had for 150 years.

All over the United States, automobiles were being manufactured in small factories, many of which had evolved from bicycle shops. They were big, hand-produced affairs which none but the rich could afford to buy or keep going. In these early days, endurance contests and racing provided the information needed for mechanical development. The first official road race was run in the vicinity of Babylon, Long Island in 1900 over a 50-mile course. Oddly enough it was won by a Riker electric in two hours, three and a half minutes. Rather a lumbering performance by any standard. In 1903 a 40-year-old mechanic named Henry Ford built a huge racing car—the "999," placed a professional bicycle rider named Barney Oldfield behind the tiller (no wheel in those days) and won a race which led directly to the formation of the Ford Motor Company. And in 1903 a Packard made the first transcontinental trip from San Francisco to New York in 52 days.

It was not until 1909, when Ford announced that henceforward he was only going to produce the Model T, that the automobile became available to the man in the street and mass production began to revolutionize American industry. As its sales increased, the price of the Model T dropped: $950, $780, $690, $600, $550, $490, $440, $360 — and finally, in 1924 to $290 which is likely to remain an all time historic low for anything with an engine in it.*

Through consolidation and acquisition the units of business and industry grew bigger and bigger. In 1901 J. Pierpont Morgan put together the U. S. Steel Corporation with a capitalization of $1,400,000,000 — a sum greater than the total national wealth in 1800.

These early days of big business were dominated by rich men rather than rich institutions. The syndicate which underwrote the U. S. Steel Corporation stock issue consisted of approximately 300 participants. Of the 26 largest 22 were individuals. Stockholdings were not spread as they are today. Before the Carnegie Steel Company was merged into the U. S. Steel Corporation, Andrew Carnegie owned over 58 per cent of the outstanding stock. In 1900 American Telephone & Telegraph had only 7,535 stockholders and no corporation in the country had over 60,000.

As a result of this concentration many individuals and

* Frederick Lewis Allen, *The Big Change.* p. 113.

small groups had a sense of personal proprietorship toward the companies which they controlled. How they ran them was nobody's business. Annual reports were apt to give the minimum of information and frequently they were omitted entirely.

There was still little government regulation of business. Even if it had been considered desirable Washington was not geared to the task. We are so used to huge government agencies that it is difficult to realize how far the pendulum has swung in less than 60 years. In 1900 total Federal expenditures were approximately a billion dollars annually. The national debt amounted to only a little over a billion and a quarter. There was no Department of Commerce or Labor, no Federal Trade Commission, no Federal Reserve System, and the entire executive staff of the White House consisted of 10 people, four of whom were doorkeepers and messengers.

On September 6, 1901, President McKinley was fatally shot at the Pan American Exposition in Buffalo. His Vice President, Theodore Roosevelt, was immediately sworn into office. He wasted no time. Within six months the United States Attorney General brought suit for the dissolution of the Northern Securities Company under the Sherman Anti-trust Act. This was a holding company created by J. Pierpont Morgan and Edward H. Harriman for the joint control of certain trans-Mississippi railroads.

The business world was stunned by the news, but actually this was to be the most important move against "big business" that Roosevelt made. What he *did* do, however, was to dramatize his views on monopolies, trusts and special privilege in a way that could be understood by the average citizen and in so doing he started a wave of reform that dominated the American scene until it was buried under the avalanche of World War I.

○◯○

Prosperity was temporarily halted in 1907 by a brief but severe "bankers' panic." Overspeculation was once again the primary cause, but behind that lay the long, competitive struggle between the new trust companies, acting as commercial banks with inadequate reserve requirements, and the more conservative and better regulated commercial banks.

The crash was precipitated by the Knickerbocker Trust Company which closed its doors on October 22nd. Runs immediately began on other trust companies. Prices collapsed on the New York Stock Exchange and interest on Stock Exchange demand loans rose to 125 per cent. The government, working in conjunction with the commercial and private banks of the City, took immediate steps to ease the situation and confidence was quickly restored.

The panic served a good purpose in that it emphasized the inelasticity of the national banking system and the need for its correction. During the following year a National Monetary Commission was appointed to make a study of the banking situation and report to Congress. As a result of this report the Federal Reserve Act was passed on December 23rd, 1913, thus, through a bit of lucky timing, putting the country's financial machinery in shape to meet the demands that would be made upon it by World War I during the next five years.

∘◯∘

New York City was engrossed in its never-ending task of trying to keep from being throttled by its own traffic and in tearing down old buildings to make room for new. The Flatiron Building, the city's first and most famous skyscraper, was completed in 1902. Digging had already started for the new subway. The Williamsburg Bridge ended the monopoly of the Brooklyn Bridge (1883) on over-water transit. Ernest Flagg's Singer Building had the temporary honor of being the highest office building in the world and two of New York's most beautiful public buildings were completed, the Pennsylvania Station and the New York Public Library. Fashionable retail shops were beginning to appear on Fifth Avenue.

Down at the Metropolitan, Enrico Caruso made his American debut before a cheering audience. Several blocks further north the new Hippodrome was mystifying its vast audiences by causing its cast to walk into a tank filled with water and apparently remain there. *The Birth of a Nation* was playing on Broadway and the side street movie houses were running a serial called *The Perils of Pauline*. Vaudeville was at its peak and the barber shop boys were working over *Sweet Adeline* ('03), *Take Me Out to the Ballgame* ('08), and *A Perfect Day* ('10).

∘◯∘

In 1904 The Bank of New York joined in commemorating the 100th anniversary of Alexander Hamilton's

94

death. In that same year the first subway train ran from Washington Heights to Brooklyn thereby linking New York into one great city. The Panama Canal cut through an isthmus and eliminated a continent for future shipping and Admiral Peary at long last reached the North Pole the hard way.

In February, 1913, the 16th Amendment to the Constitution was adopted authorizing Congress to impose taxes on personal incomes, but its significance was obscured by the outbreak of World War I the following year. The change which the New Year's Eve revelers of 1899 had anticipated was at hand.

CHAPTER V

Changing America
1914-1950

To most Americans the outbreak of World War I was like an explosion shattering the drowsy quiet of a midsum-

1914-1929 mer afternoon. Absorbed in the enjoyment, or the antici- pation, of his summer vacation, the average man had not been paying much attention to events in Europe. Even if he had, the chances are they would have seemed remote, protected as he was by two oceans.

Even the tourists in France and Belgium failed to sense the crisis until many of them were awakened from their morning sleep by the clatter of hobnailed boots and the rumble of artillery wheels in the streets below.

In the United States the crowds stared unbelievingly at the bulletin boards. The New York Stock Exchange and the Cotton Exchange closed. As Europe sold American securities, gold flowed out of the country and loans for domestic purposes became increasingly difficult to obtain.

During the final weeks of July, 1914, the officers of The Bank of New York had become convinced that war was inevitable and had sold $2,000,000 of securities, which put the Bank in a position to meet all normal demands made upon it during the height of the crisis. Having lived through four wars it was beginning to acquire a sixth sense.

After a few anxious months and with the help of the Federal Reserve System, which began operations on November 16th, the country struggled through the dislocations brought on by the outbreak of the war and found itself rather unexpectedly in the midst of a boom as the Allies turned to the United States for raw materials and food supplies. The Bank of New York was the long-established agent and correspondent of a number of important London banks and private bankers, as a result of which its business increased greatly during this period.

In spite of our declared neutrality, the United States sensed the inevitable and steps were immediately taken to strengthen our national defenses. At first opinion was divided, but after the sinking of the *Lusitania* in May, 1915, the dissident voices all but ceased and a unified America began to prepare in earnest for an unwanted war.

We entered the conflict on April 6, 1917. As had been the case in former national crises, the Bank extended itself to the limit of its ability to support the Government's financial program. It subscribed, for its own account and for its customers, to approximately $45,000,000 of war loan bonds and purchased short term Treasury Certificates in excess of $46,000,000 — an excellent record for an organization which at the end of the war had only 10 officers and 123 other employees.

○◯○

As the guns fell silent at 11 o'clock on the morning of November 11, 1918, the people of the United States discovered that they were living in a new world. Their country had suddenly become the largest creditor nation. New York was now the international money center rather than London. One-half of the world's gold supply was in our vaults. By 1920 the cost of living, based on 1913 as parity, stood at 208.5; and wages, on the same basis, stood at 234. Income and estate taxes had been increased tremendously during the war. Rents were rising. The genie of inflation had been let out of the bottle. No one would succeed in re-bottling him from that day to this.

A small segment of the population had grown rich during the war years and almost everyone was receiving more money than he had been before 1914. The golden Twenties were dawning — a decade that will be vividly remembered by all who lived through it as the most restless, reckless and colorful period of the current century.

As we recall the outstanding participants in this fast-moving pageant it is hard to believe that 30 years or more have slipped by since most of them stepped out of the spotlight. It seems like such a short time ago that we were reading F. Scott Fitzgerald's *This Side of Paradise* and Sinclair Lewis' *Main Street*. It was "only yesterday" that we watched Bill Tilden and Helen Wills in their tennis prime at Forest Hills, cheered for Babe Ruth and Bobby Jones and followed the exploits of Man o' War, and Gertrude Ederle.

Lindbergh's flight seems further removed in time, but that is because of the phenomenal development of aviation in the intervening years. It is somewhat of a jolt nonetheless to realize that in three years this young man, who won the heart of a nation at 25, will be celebrating his 60th birthday.

There was so much going on in the big tent that it was hard to focus on any one act. The Boston police strike was catapulting an inarticulate governor into the White House. The still unsolved Wall Street explosion had shocked the world. It was the period of rising skirts and dropping waistlines, of day-by-day-in-every-way Coué, mah jongg, the black bottom and the Charleston, the Scopes trial, flag-pole sitters, Tut-ankh-amen's tomb and John Held's long-legged "flappers."

In the background of these varied happenings, developments were afoot, both mechanical and social, destined to change the life of every American. At the head of the list was the automobile, but of almost equal importance was the debut of radio and the coming of age of the motion picture. Prohibition contributed its bit and stock market speculation was paving the way for some radical innovations during the Thirties.

o◯o

In 1915 there were less than 2,500,000 cars registered in the United States. By 1920 the number had risen to 9,000,000. In 1925 it was nearly 20,000,000 and by 1930, over 26,500,000.

These figures tell the story. The automobile was on its way to transforming the habits as well as the face of the nation. By the end of 1929 it had ended rural isolation. It had made a shambles out of our cities and towns. It had revolutionized suburban life. It had made the approaches to our populated areas into neon-lighted nightmares, *but* it had given the American family a mobility that it had never had before.

Automobiles were no longer being hand-produced in former bicycle shops. A relatively few large companies were beginning to dominate the field. In his book *Our Times** Mark Sullivan notes that, out of 1,000 automobile companies which had been started since the beginning of the industry, only 15 remained in operation by 1925. They were:

Haynes	1896	Pierce-Arrow	1901
Olds	1897	Cadillac	1902
Studebaker	1898	Overland	1902
Locomobile	1899	Packard	1902
Franklin	1900	Buick	1903
Peerless	1900	Ford	1903
Stearns	1900	Maxwell	1904
Apperson	1901		

Only five have survived until today, three of which were divisions of General Motors when this list was compiled.

In spite of its phenomenal acceptance the automobile and its adjuncts developed slowly. In the Twenties the country roads were atrocious, gas stations were few and far between, and if you had a date in a neighboring town you were wise not to put on your good suit until you arrived for you might be changing a tire on the way. Every motorist was his own mechanic and his running-

* Mark Sullivan, *Our Times*, Vol. I. p. 484.

board tool box was something to be cherished, for nobody knew better than he that when the comedians sang, "You've got to get out, get out and get under," they meant it.

Our cities, villages and countryside had grown up around a horse civilization. The streets of the cities had never been intended for the volume of traffic that a motorized world was beginning to turn loose in them. The villages became bottlenecks through whose elm-bordered Main Streets the Sunday traffic edged irritably until the frustrated City Fathers chopped down the elms and doubled their police forces in a vain attempt to relieve a situation which merely grew worse. Out in the country the old winding dirt roads were widened and straightened, then widened and straightened again only to be swamped by increased traffic as soon as they were reopened.

It was a period of adaptation, of forcing old things to serve new ends. It could have happened in no other way. Small changes brought more cars. More cars made further changes either profitable or essential. And so it went until we reached a stage where it became obvious that nothing would suffice but a complete rebuilding, designed to meet the requirements of an age that had broken with its past completely and forever.

◦◯◦

Hand in hand with the development of the automobile went the radio and the motion picture. Immediately after Dr. Frank Conrad put on the first radio broadcast in 1920 the industry started to bloom. As thousands bought "crystal" sets and "earmuffs" the blossoming continued so rapidly that within 10 years annual radio sales were over three-quarters of a billion dollars.

The motion picture industry was considerably older but it did not come into its own until the "star" system was developed about 1920. From that time on a relatively small group of people received an adulation from the American public usually reserved for national heroes. Charlie Chaplin duck-footing through *The Kid* and *The Gold Rush*, Sheik Valentino in *The Four Horsemen of the Apocalypse*, Mary Pickford and Doug, the comics Harold Lloyd and Buster Keaton, the Gish girls, Gloria Swanson, Greta Garbo and Theda Bara (in honor of whom the word "vamp" was coined) — all enjoyed the complete lack of privacy which is the American hallmark of fame.

o◯o

On January 16, 1920, the National Prohibition Enforcement Act went into effect. It was an extraordinary thing to have happened, for at no time in its history had the United States been less in tune with reform. The hard core of Europe's political leaders had been revealed to a disillusioned nation as the peace negotiations bogged down and as a result the idealism engendered by the war had been replaced by a spirit of cynicism.

Instead of curbing the nation's drinking habits, Prohibition initiated thousands into the fine art of cocktail mixing. The youth of the country was prepared — even eager — to become a "lost" generation. Prohibition was just what was needed to give the movement impetus.

As the decade progressed a wave of stock speculation swept the country. As stock prices continued to rise and profits were realized, spending increased. More and more people were attracted to what seemed to them a gold mine, open to the public — people of limited means, with no knowledge of the market, who only wanted to make some sorely needed money and then, of course, "get out."

By the fall of 1929, brokers' loans had reached the unprecedented figure of $8,000,000,000. On September 3rd, American Telephone & Telegraph stock sold at $335 a share, General Electric at $396 and United States Steel at $261. Early in September the market broke sharply, recovered partially and then, on October 23rd, began a precipitous drop in which there frequently were no bids for active stocks. On October 24th, sales were just under 13,000,000 shares with standard stocks suffering enormous drops between sales. A banking group formed an emergency pool, but to no avail. On October 29th sales reached 16,419,000 and it became apparent to all that the golden, colorful Twenties had come to an end.

o◯o

The Bank of New York had been through too many periods of "boom and bust," too many "aftermaths of battle," to be swayed by the mounting hysteria of the Twenties. Shortly after the end of World War I, however, it became obvious that, in an expanding economy, a larger capital structure was needed in order to serve properly the commercial needs of the Bank's customers and to further protect its rapidly growing deposits.

On May 9, 1922, President Herbert L. Griggs presented to his Board a proposal for a merger of The Bank of New York and the New York Life Insurance and Trust Company. One result of such a merger would be to increase the capital of the Bank from $2,000,000 to $4,000,000.

The proposal was approved by the Board and submitted to the stockholders of both banks by whom it was promptly ratified. In July, 1922, The Bank of New York gave up its status as a national bank and became a state bank, changing its title to The Bank of New York and Trust Company.

Edwin G. Merrill, who had been President of the New York Life Insurance and Trust Company, became president of the merged bank. In addition to increasing its capital structure, the merger brought to the Bank an established and important trust business. The clients of the New York Life Insurance and Trust Company had been, for the most part, members of old New York families and institutions with large security portfolios. Its fiduciary business had been conducted on a highly personalized basis, the affairs of each customer being given detailed attention by an officer. The Bank of New York had been conducting its banking affairs along similar lines for 138 years so that from this point of view the merger was a natural one in which the officers of each bank merely continued to work together along the lines they had followed so successfully as separate institutions.

It became immediately obvious that new and larger quarters were essential to enable the Bank to continue its growth. In 1925, President Merrill succeeded in purchasing from the National City Bank the property immediately adjoining its building to the east, thus giving the Bank frontage on Wall Street of approximately 100 feet.

Plans were drawn for a new building. On June 18, 1927, the cornerstone of the old building, laid in 1856, was removed. As is so frequently the case with cornerstones, its contents were described as "disappointing."

The new building was completed and occupied during the early part of 1929. Its 32 stories provided ample room for future expansion and its skillful adaptation of Colonial architecture to the requirements of modern business would have undoubtedly pleased that most modern of its founders — Alexander Hamilton.

In the meantime a branch office had been established at Madison Avenue and 63rd Street, immediately after the merger, and in 1927 the capital of the Bank was increased from $4,000,000 to $6,000,000 by the declaration of a 50 per cent stock dividend.

The war had brought the old order to an end. The world of William Dean Howells, McKinley, Richard Harding Davis and Horatio Alger, Jr., had gone forever. Modern America had emerged from the ashes of conflict. The Bank of New York was orienting itself to meet these new conditions.

EXIT THE OLD ORDER

Most people failed at first to gauge the magnitude of the depression which followed the stock market crash of 1929-1941

1929. Nor did they suspect that the desperate, uncoordinated attempts to stem the tide of economic disaster would result in a complete change in their way of living, a change in the course of which the traditional policy of *laissez faire* on the part of government would be replaced by a system of Federal controls that would have been considered by a pre-depression world as the end of personal liberty.

President Hoover struggled to restore order, but he was operating within the framework of established precedent and with due regard for "rugged individualism." His efforts were swept away like debris before a spring flood and they probably would have been regardless of what methods he might have used, for the early force of the downswing was almost irresistable.

When Franklin D. Roosevelt was elected president in the fall of 1932, unemployment was estimated at between 13 and 17 million, 1,400 banks had failed, commercial failures had reached the staggering total of 32,000, farmers in the Middle West were in open revolt against the foreclosure of their farms, and national income had dropped from $80,000,000,000 to $40,000,000,000.

By the time Roosevelt took office in March, 1933, there were 20 states where bank moratoria had been established or where the banks were operating under special regulations. On the day of his inauguration New York State and Illinois declared a bank holiday, thus closing the country's most important stock and commodity markets.

What happened during the first hundred days of the new administration is familiar to most. A general bank moratorium was declared immediately. This was followed by a bewildering series of bills which were passed, all but unread, by an inflation-minded and jittery Congress. In a series of legal steps the gold standard was abandoned, crop controls were imposed, young men began marching off to the woods under the banner of the CCC, money was appropriated for a huge public works program, relief funds were distributed on an unprecedented scale, the government went into the power and finance business, security transactions were placed under rigid controls and that ill-fated child of the Brain Trust, the NRA, stamped its blue eagle on almost every phase of American business.

It was a mammoth pump-priming, so enormous that it made little difference if a good bit of water missed the pump and spilled on the ground; a legislative free-for-all in which one hand sought recovery by creating scarcity while the other strove for the same end by creating abundance; an alphabetical nightmare in which agency was piled upon agency until the lines of authority disappeared in the tangle.

Securities listed on the New York Stock Exchange had decreased in value in the amount of $40,000,000,000. During December, 1930, the Bank of the United States, with 62 branches and deposits of approximately $200,000,000 closed its doors. Smaller banks were going down by the hundreds and some states were left without any banking facilities whatever.

On March 31, 1931, during the most difficult days of the crisis, John C. Traphagen became the 17th president of the Bank. With his calm wisdom and sound judgment

he guided it safely through the longest and deepest depression in our history. It emerged from its ordeal not only unharmed but with its official staff strengthened, its deposits increased and its field of activities materially enlarged.

One of the new president's first acts was to expand the commercial and trust business of the Bank. He established an investment counsel division which has since become nationally known and he set up a security research division designed to serve the particular requirements of the Bank's investment accounts. To assist him in this development he brought into the Bank a number of young men many of whom are still active as senior officers.

The majority of people go about their day-to-day business regardless of the state of the Union or of what may be happening in Washington, London or Tokyo. This was particularly striking in 1931 when, with the national economy disintegrating all about them, worried citizens from Portland, Maine, to Portland, Oregon, spent hours of their enforced idleness and thousands of dollars daily, knocking golf balls across tiny synthetic fairways, rolling them over little arched bridges and through drainpipes, or crouching tensely over pocket-handkerchief putting greens. With the coming of twilight they gathered about their radios to listen to two unknown men unfold the trials of Amos and Andy and when Bobby Jones returned from England with the British Open and Amateur championships under his arm, he was smothered with ticker tape on which was printed the ominous record of a steadily falling market.

The faint rumblings of a future storm went unnoted. While Japan was making final preparations for the invasion of Manchuria the world watched Post and Gatty as they readied the *Winnie Mae* for its globe-girdling journey. Katherine Cornell was playing to packed houses from a Wimpole Street sofa. Pretty girls in their age-old quest for the bizarre and the unbecoming were proudly wearing unadorned felt hats resembling German helmets, while Rudy Vallee swooned the teen-age world by announcing somewhat incongruously that life was just a bowl of cherries.

During December, 1933, the nation was given a Christmas present in the repeal of Prohibition. It prepared for an old time celebration only to discover that the only ingredients available were of the familiar bathtub variety which were no longer acceptable now that they were legal.

The spirit of the times was changing. Man was losing ground in the age-old battle of the sexes. Quietly, relentlessly women were moving into the smoking cars, the bars (renamed "cocktail lounges" for their benefit) and even into the hitherto sacred precincts of men's clubs. Remembering the phrase in the marriage service, ". . . till death us do part," they were accompanying their mates to the country club, standing loyally beside them in the trout streams, following them down the ski trails and even going along with them occasionally on business trips. Feminism was taking unforeseen directions.

∘◯∘

By the end of 1934, the New Deal honeymoon was over. The pump priming of early 1933 had been reasonably effective. It had created jobs and increased the Federal Reserve Board's Adjusted Index of Industrial Production from 59 to 100. Since then, however, the economy, like a weary swimmer fighting too swift a current, had been slipping back. Unemployment was still high, the NRA was not working according to expectations, there was only one direction for Roosevelt to take. Like Alice's Red Queen he could only move faster and faster in order to stay at least in the same place. The CWA, the WPA, the PWA, Social Security and a dozen other projects followed one another in overlapping succession.

Through the tumult and the shouting it was becoming evident, as the years passed, that despite the billions spent on destroying the depression it was still very much alive. As a matter of fact it never was conquered until the Germans marched into Poland in the fall of 1939. At that time, the Federal Reserve Board's Adjusted Index stood at 102 — only two points higher than in June, 1933. According to the estimates of the National Industrial Conference Board, 9,500,000 people were still unemployed. The United States had become a subsidizing nation. The WPA was beginning to look like a permanent institution. The virus of boondoggling had crept over the land and those who observed the groups of apathetic men leaning on their shovels beside the highways realized that it was far from good either for the country or for those unhappily involved.

In the meanwhile the war clouds continued to gather. While those dissimilar apostles of security, Dr. Townsend and Huey Long, sought to make every man a subsidized king, while Jim Braddock was snatching the heavyweight boxing championship from Max Baer, and John Marquand was writing *The Late George Apley,* the forces of totalitarianism were quietly consolidating their positions in Germany, Italy and Japan.

In May, 1935, Mussolini, chin out and trumpets flourishing, invaded Ethiopia, the League of Nations indicating displeasure. A year later Hitler moved into the Rhineland and civil war broke out in Spain. In 1937 Japan attacked China and in 1938 Hitler's tanks rumbled into Austria.

America was shocked, but its people, struggling to emerge from a depression and to clear away the wreckage of a hurricane, wanted no more war. They thought of these distressing events in terms of military aggression rather than as a new force about to challenge their fundamental concepts of liberty. They looked gratefully at the oceans which isolated them from all these deplorable events, passed a Neutrality Act and turned back to their labors.

We had been drawn into the European vortex once. Never again!

In 1937-38 there was a sharp depression. Once more stock prices declined at a rate comparable to 1929. With a vivid recollection of those dreadful days, business and individuals began immediately to retrench, thus accelerating deflation. In 1937 Roosevelt had at least begun to *talk* about a balanced budget. By the end of 1938 all such ideas were swept aside and dollars by the hundreds of millions began to flow once more into the leaky old pump which somehow refused to stay primed.

o◯o

In December, 1938, the Munich Conference yielded the Sudetanland and most of the Czech fortresses to Hitler. The people of America sensed at last the true nature of what was happening overseas. Jack Benny, Bing Crosby and Charlie McCarthy could still make them laugh but they couldn't erase the sinking feeling that the world was flying apart. Benny Goodman might tootle his lungs out, middle-aged people shorten their days trying to dance the Big Apple and Snow White's dwarfs provide a momentary escape outlet, but over the horizon there was always the remembered glow of burning farmhouses and the rumble of iron shod wheels.

On September 1, 1939, Hitler's armies marched into Poland and World War II had begun. At the New York World's Fair crowds continued to mill about in the "Court of Peace," but they knew that "peace in our time" had been merely the wish-thinking of a tired old man.

As France, Belgium and Holland fell before the mechanized power of the German armies, they looked on with numb incredulity. As they watched Britain fighting for its life they knew that if it fell the United States would be next in line. Neutrality melted in the heat from London's burning buildings. America began to rearm.

For a time it seemed as if we might merely drift into the war, but an explosive impetus came from an unexpected quarter. On December 7, 1941, Japan struck without warning at Pearl Harbor and for the second time in a quarter of a century we were fighting for our lives in a world-wide conflict which we had mistakenly thought was no concern of ours.

The Atlantic and Pacific barriers, which had protected us for three centuries, had disappeared overnight.

GLOBAL WAR AND PROBLEMS OF GLOBAL PEACE

1941-1950 Before the columns of acrid smoke had ceased to rise from the stricken battleships at Pearl Harbor, the people of the United States had unified behind a single purpose — to win a war that had been thrust upon them and to win it as decisively and quickly as possible.

American industry had been turning out war material for two years, and peacetime conscription had already provided an army of a million and a half men, but the task of putting production on a full wartime basis overnight was nonetheless a tremendous one.

There was a hidden asset in the industrial picture, however, which was not fully appreciated at the time. During the depression of the 1930's American business had achieved an efficiency greater than it realized. As sales volume had declined during those heartbreaking years, thousands of companies had been forced either to reduce operating costs or go out of business. Now they were suddenly thrown into high gear. Their orders were to turn out equipment and to disregard cost. The steps taken in desperation during the '30s became the basis for a production miracle in the '40s.

114

By the time Japan surrendered in August, 1945, the United States had produced almost 300,000 planes, 86,000 tanks, 3,000,000 machine guns, 55,000,000 tons of merchant shipping and thousands of other items in such vast quantities that, in addition to filling our own pipe lines, we were able to supply many of the needs of Britain and to some extent those of Russia.

Produce the goods. Never mind the expense. By the end of 1943, expenditures were five times as great as they had been at the peak of World War I. During 1944 government spending reached 95 billions and the following year it topped 98 billions. As a result the national debt rose from 43 billions in 1940 to 258 billions in 1945, but the armament had been produced and the war had been won.

It was a war fought with savage efficiency, and with little of the crusading spirit that characterized World War I. This was no war to end war, or to make the world safe for democracy. Gone were the marching songs — *It's a Long Way to Tipperary*, *Over There* and *Pack Up Your Troubles in Your Old Kit Bag*. It was a dirty job which had to be done. All the average GI craved was to finish it off and go home.

On the domestic front, as employment hit new peaks and overtime made pay envelopes bulge, a wave of prosperity swept the land. While people were rationing their car mileage, cutting down on cigarettes and devising substitutes for sugar and coffee, the demand for luxury goods became insatiable. Fur coats and jewelry sold faster than

they had during the Twenties, restaurants were jammed—
the more expensive the greater the jam — and it was impossible to get seats for the good shows at any price.

Financing industry and helping the government to raise
its enormous war loans imposed a heavy load on the banks.
They worked together in the closest cooperation with the
government, selling war bonds, making huge sums available to war industry either directly or through V Loans,
selling government obligations and taking them into their
portfolios, and contributing the services of their depleted
staffs for hundreds of wartime activities.

By September 2, 1945, it was all over. The end came
so suddenly, so melodramatically, that it was almost un-
realistic to a world conditioned by six years of tension.
Within the span of 109 days Mussolini had been murdered
by the hands that a short time before had greeted him so
eagerly with the Fascist salute; Hitler lay dead in a rubble-
strewn bunker; Germany had surrendered unconditionally,
its seemingly invincible war machine smashed to bits; and
the first atom bomb had exploded over Japan, bringing an
immediate end to the war in the Pacific.

The country faced the post-war readjustment, wonder-
ing uneasily what was going to happen, now that the pres-
sure was suddenly removed. Was reaction inevitable?
People's minds went back apprehensively to 1929. Somewhat to their surprise nothing happened. The United
States went right on being prosperous. The United Nations, begun as a military alliance during the war, had now
become a permanent body, a guarantee, the world hoped,

against future wars. From coast to coast people settled back for a period of well-earned relaxation.

And then, slowly, unwillingly, there came the realization that Russia — a country so far away that most Americans had never even taken it seriously up to that time — a land associated in the average mind with revolutions, droshkies, the Volga Boat Song, Czars and squatting gypsy dancers — appeared for some unaccountable reason, to be bent on global domination.

Overnight our plans for relaxation had to be abandoned. Instead, America found itself the somewhat uncertain leader of the free world. The wealth generated by World War II must be used for armament, for the Marshall Plan, for emergencies such as the Berlin airlift, to a large extent for NATO and for a dozen other measures aimed at maintaining a worldwide state of preparedness to meet a threat that everyone prayed would never materialize. Our frontiers had moved outward once more and were now in the Arctic and the Antarctic, throughout the seven seas and, as time went on, they extended into outer space itself.

In New York a building boom had commenced, destined to change the familiar face of the city. Faster and faster became the tempo of the City's life, more and more congested its streets. Hotels were jammed. Transportation difficult. People didn't write letters any more, they telephoned. And at Christmastime the stores were so crowded with buyers that it was almost impossible to buy. The magnitude of Federal spending had suddenly made thrift seem picayune.

Diplomats and statesmen shuttled restlessly about the globe, attending profitless conferences. The Republic of Israel was born. Tito revolted against the Russian Bear and to everyone's surprise continued to prosper. As Nationalist China collapsed, Communist China moved in quietly behind it. NATO became a healthy reality, and around the world the seismographs recorded the explosion of Russia's first atom bomb. It was a radio commentators' heaven.

On April 30, 1948, The Bank of New York merged with The Fifth Avenue Bank which for 73 years had occupied offices on the corner of Fifth Avenue and 44th Street. At this time Albert C. Simmonds, Jr. became President of the Bank and John C. Traphagen, who had held that office for 17 years, became Chairman of the Board.

Of the numerous bank mergers which took place during the post-war years this was perhaps the most natural. The Bank of New York had never had a midtown office. The Fifth Avenue Bank had no Wall Street office. Both banks had a national reputation for soundness, conservatism and personalized service. Both banks had always believed that there was a need in New York for a medium-sized institution large enough to take care of normal commercial requirements, yet small enough to insure the attention of senior officers to the affairs of its customers.

The merger was an outstanding success from the day the new bank opened for business under the temporary title of The Bank of New York and Fifth Avenue Bank. The old brownstone buildings formerly occupied by The Fifth

Avenue Bank were eventually replaced by one of the most modern office buildings in the City. As one enters the new midtown office it seems a long way back to the first home of The Bank of New York in the old Walton House or to the converted brownstones which housed The Fifth Avenue Bank for so many years.

CHAPTER VI

Threshold of a New World
1950-1959

It is easier to appraise the past than the present. In the former case time is apt to do the appraising for us. We are too familiar with the details which make up the current scene to distinguish between the unimportant and the significant. The only comment we can make with certainty about today's world is that its dominant note is uncertainty.

It is an uncertainty created in large part by discoveries and technological developments which have come too fast to be assimilated. They have already changed the life and the thinking of every living person, but it is a change which has only begun. Its ultimate direction is still concealed in the pages of tomorrow's history.

The last ten years have been crowded with events which are bound to shape the future history of the United States. Some of the most important have been taking place, quietly and unheralded, in the research laboratories of the nation where dedicated men have been developing new methods of controlling the hitherto uncontrollable and discovering new sources of energy, new materials, new ways of penetrating realms which no one has ever before dreamed of invading.

THE BANK'S NEW
FIFTH AVENUE
OFFICE

On every side the signs are multiplying that man is on the verge of a major breakthrough into a greater understanding of the world in which he has lived so long — an understanding which might well release him from his age-old bondage into a freedom of which he has never before dreamed.

It is a "threshold" moment in history and from the point of view of The Bank of New York a particularly dramatic one on which to celebrate its 175th birthday. The Bank has lived and grown with the Republic since the day it was founded. Washington took the oath of office within a few hundred yards of its first home. From this beginning it has watched the nation grow to its present might.

By constantly refusing to be caught in the speculative currents which have periodically swept the country, it has ridden unharmed through panics and depressions. By refusing to give way to fear during the darker days of our national history it has been able to steer a steady course through every crisis.

During April, 1930, it published a statement in the leading New York newspapers under the title "A Declaration of Principles" which said in part:

"There is a real place in New York for conservatively managed banks and trust companies of moderate size, where customers may have easy access to and personal acquaintance with the senior officers. . . ."

There is no reason to amend that statement today. The Bank is constantly modifying its services and installing new mechanized equipment to meet the requirements of an expanding economy. Regardless of change, however, it still considers the maintenance of "the personal touch" to be one of its most important obligations.

During December, 1957, John C. Traphagen retired. He was succeeded as Chairman of the Board by Albert C. Simmonds, Jr. who, during his decade as President, had greatly increased the commercial business of the Bank, streamlined its operations, strengthened its staff and who was largely responsible for its new Fifth Avenue office at 44th Street. Donald M. Elliman, who had been head of that office, became the Bank's eighteenth President.

At the end of 175 years, the leadership of The Bank of New York lies in the hands of relatively young men attuned to the rapidly changing conditions which characterize the modern business world. Backed as these men are by a loyal and experienced staff, the Bank looks forward to the eighth quarter century of its existence, confident that the qualities implanted by the founders, which have enabled it to meet with honor the challenges of the past, will continue to sustain it in the years which lie ahead.

X

DLV 2/2 Ex